"In these uncertain times, it's important to have clear, specific str-- -es on how to manage your business. John and K-- have ---- --- -- nonsense guide that will help you ach-- --- --- --- --- cially liked their guidance on goal settin--
—Kathy Parks,

"John and Ken cut through all the noise and confusion that exist in the business world. The process outlined in this book is clear and concise and will drive measurable results. The hardest thing for a manager to do is to get a team of individuals moving in the same direction, and this is the playbook to make that happen."

—Scott Dahlquist, VP, Major International Forest Products Company

"If you want to develop a high-performance team, this would be the first book I would recommend."

—Tim Riley, founder, Door to Door Storage

"John Cioffi and Ken Willig gave us valuable direction on running our business. I am glad to see they have a book that condenses their precious lore into a form that one can open up and dig into."

—Royal Robbins, founder, Royal Robbins, Inc.

"The management principles and techniques described in this book, and taught to us by Ken Willig, were the main reasons that the new owners felt empowered and knowledgeable to lead the company forward, and the company continues to prosper and be of value to its clients and its new owners to this day."

—Johan H. Jansen, founder, Jansen Combustion and Boiler Technologies, Inc.

"If I had to choose the one thing that made the difference between what made our company become a national leader in our industry or a just statistic, it would be Willig and Cioffi's coaching on how to manage for success. **6 Habits of Highly Effective Managers** describes a way of life for any business. John and Ken have hit a home run with this book. For those striving to be the best of the best, personally and professionally, this is your bible."

—John Hennessy, CEO and president, Nuprecon, Inc.

"This is a very practical guide for leaders of all organizations who want to be better at executing. The authors have a unique ability to convey coaching ideas using anecdotes and real business stories."

—Tim Leybold, CFO, ICO Global Ltd

"In today's turbulent economy, managers need a concise vision and strategy in order to be successful. Ken and John have detailed valuable *directions to obtain that vision and strategy. Their book is a must read for anyone who is serious about managing people."*

—W.R. Nath, president and CEO, HOC Industries, Inc.

"John and Ken have set forth the managerial tenets that will powerfully enable any company to compete. Setting the right vision, connecting to the right customers, empowering the right employees under constant and consistent management will yield the right results."

—Jonathan C. Crane, former chief strategy officer and executive VP, MCI, Inc.

"By putting strategic planning in the context of process management driven by constant feedback, they help us free up hundreds of hours of writing plans that sit on the shelf. This is a must read for CEOs and managers who want to become CEO's."

— Merrill J. Oster, founder, Oster Communications and Pinnacle Forum America

"We have used the important information presented in **6 Habits** *in our non-profit organization, and it's a major reason why we have been so successful in growing and increasing our impact."*

—Dann Mead Smith, president, Washington Policy Center

"John and Ken have organized what all business execs need to know. I get weary with theory. So this hands-on, practical, to-the-point style of writing by those who have been successful in managing for results will get lots of attention."

—Robert C. Andringa, PhD, managing partner, The Andringa Group

*"If your goal is to do the right things in your company to be successful then start now by reading—***6 Habits of Highly Successful Managers***. Today, more than ever before, managers must be focused on setting the right goals for their companies and employees, and you simply cannot run a successful business without the information in this book."*

—Bill Williams Jr., founder/chairman, Telect, Inc.

"6 Habits of Highly Successful Managers is a breath of fresh air giving us a new way of structuring for success. This is a must-read for the president of every company and for everyone who calls themselves a manager."

—Roger Roberson, former chairman and CEO, Roberson Transportation, Inc.

*"***6 Habits of Highly Successful Managers** *is critical reading for business leaders in today's economic environment. It will help you develop quality leadership techniques, provides insights that many other business books don't...."*

—Steven D Whiteman, Chairman of the Board, Unify Corporation

Highly
Successful
Managers

John Cioffi and Ken Willig

CAREER
PRESS

Pompton Plains, NJ

6 Habits of Highly Successful Managers

Edited by Kate Henches
Typeset by *the*BookDesigners
Cover design by Jeff Piasky
Printed in the U.S.A.

To order this title, please call toll-free 1-800-CAREER-1 (NJ and Canada: 201-848-0310) to order using VISA or MasterCard, or for further information on books from Career Press.

The Career Press, Inc.
220 West Parkway, Unit 12
Pompton Plains, NJ 07444
www.careerpress.com

Library of Congress Cataloging-in-Publication Data
Cioffi, John.
6 habits of highly successful managers / by John Cioffi and Ken Willig.
p. cm.
Includes bibliographical references and index.
ISBN 978-1-60163-137-4 -- ISBN 978-1-60163-690-4 (ebook) 1. Management. 2.
Leadership. I. Willig, Ken. II. Title. III.
Title: Six habits of highly successful managers.
HD31.C533 2011
658.4--dc22
2010034226

Dedication

To our clients: We are forever grateful to all of our clients for your trust and confidence. You allow us to speak candidly, encouragingly, and, at times, critically. We love our role as coaches, and we treasure the opportunities you have given us to participate in your successes.

Our association with you has always resulted in measurable changes to your company as well as to us, and in some cases we have forged fabulous friendships which we treasure greatly. You've taught us much of what we know about how to create successful businesses, and we learned something valuable from each of you. Thank you!

Acknowledgments

First, we are forever grateful to all our clients for teaching us much of what we know about how to create successful businesses. We love our role as coaches, and we treasure the opportunities you have given us to participate in your successes. We've learned something valuable from each of you.

Many of our friends, colleagues, and family members provided us with advice and critique early in the development of this book as well as during its production. We are enormously grateful to all of you.

Helping us to put this book in your hands were Ellen Neuborne, who assisted us in navigating the publishing industry, and Cynthia Zigmund, our wonderful literary agent, who provided us with startlingly good advice and critique and found the right publisher for us at Career Press.

Finally, though certainly not least, we are thankful to our wives for their patience and understanding. They believed in us and in our goal of bringing our ideas to the printed page and thus to a broader audience.

Dec 2010

Best Wishes

CONTENTS

Introduction 11

CHAPTER 1: Set goals all the time 15

Company goals come in three flavors 16
Don't pick up nails 38
Say no to the hamster wheel 40

CHAPTER 2: Focus on the process, not a plan 43

Most businesses don't have a plan 44
The process is more important than the plan 46
Creating a planning process 49
Survival of the fittest ideas 69

CHAPTER 3: Coach the right people 73

Never try to teach a pig to sing 75
Matching people to the position 81
Hire the right person, not the right resume 103

CHAPTER 4: Serve the right customer 109

Define the right customers 112
Create the right strategies for your right customers ... 115
Create a sales process to secure and serve your right customers 129
Create an operations process to serve your right customers 135
Constantly build the culture 140

CHAPTER 5: Empower your entire team 143

How can you empower your team? 144
Management would be easy if you didn't have to deal with people . 146
Enabling real empowerment 148
Goals and boundaries 148
Conditions for empowerment 157
Wide boulevards, high curbs 168
The process as a diagnostic tool 168

CHAPTER 6: Do the right things right 171

A system of managing 172
The Goal Management Team (GMT) 177
The six tools 179

APPENDIX A: Using your financial statements to generate more
profit and more cash 197

APPENDIX B: Business plan outline and guidance 207

APPENDIX C: The interviewing process: one of a manager's
most critical activities 225

APPENDIX D: The sales process: an example step 235

APPENDIX E: Improving communications 239

RECOMMENDED READING 243

INDEX 249

ABOUT THE AUTHORS 255

Introduction

I n today's business world, information is generated in massive volumes and transmitted at lightning speed. Owners and managers are inundated with a mighty river of opinions, data, and ideas on achieving success and avoiding failures. What are owners and managers to do? What advice should they take, or ignore?

Because of the sheer volume of information and the many variations of similar-sounding advice, owners and managers may conclude that it's just easier to ignore it all. Or perhaps they listen to a friend who recommends this notion or that one.

We've looked at many successful companies and read countless stories of successful and unsuccessful companies across decades of varying economic conditions. We've concluded that there are some key and basic activities that managers can undertake to improve greatly their chances of success. These activities are basic building blocks. They are neither faddish nor outdated, but enduring in their effectiveness.

We've identified six of these activities. We call them *6 Habits of Highly Successful Managers*.

Using the Six Habits will compel you to do the right things (good leadership) as well as to do things right (good management). In effect, the Six Habits provide you with a road map for doing the right things right. They also help you avoid the other three options, which are roads to failure.

Doing the Right Things Right

Many managers use one or more of these habits at one time or another. For example, after a long period of aimlessness, a manager may decide to define her division's goals and to construct a plan for the coming year. Another manager might adopt some effective management practices in response to a period of chaos, while yet another might decide to improve his operations by "weeding out the dead wood" and replacing the non-performers with "folks who can do the job."

Unfortunately, and predictably, these measures alone often are unsuccessful. And this sometimes leads managers to conclude that they are inherently ineffective.

For example, consider the manager who just decided to set some goals and make a plan for the coming year. Without the discipline and accountability to actually implement the plan, her division almost certainly will not achieve its goals. Perhaps even worse, the manager will initially raise expectations only to leave her team demoralized and disillusioned by inaction or lack of success. The result will be a team that would have been better off if no goals had been set and no plans made! At least the day-to-day "muddling through" would have had the comfort of an established routine.

Companies that use the Six Habits in a consistent and habitual way create a compelling environment for success. There's only one hitch: You actually have to do this stuff. And make no mistake, being consistent and habitual in applying these practices is not easy for everyone. It takes discipline and commitment.

We've been asked if a company can be successful without employing the Six Habits. In other words, does their use create an exclusive environment for success?

We believe that some companies can achieve success through other means. For example, some highly intuitive high-control managers can create successful companies without empowered employees, without goals that are known to the employees, and without a widely known plan to reach those goals. Unfortunately, these individuals must be present at all times to ensure that things are always being done the "right way" (that is, their way). When these high-control managers leave the company, it often declines or fails.

Conversely, when a company employs the Six Habits effectively, it creates systematic processes that engage everyone in achieving the company's goals. In effect, the firm creates a culture of achievement and accountability that builds upon the collective abilities of the team to ensure the firm's success.

This book includes several means of illustrating our point of view. These include actual client stories, plain narratives, and a composite story of a construction-related company owned by "Mike." Mike's "voice" in these stories is remarkably similar to the voices of owners we have known through recent years, and the points illustrated in the brief stories of Mike's company are common to many businesses across industries and across the country.

An important premise of the Six Habits is that many managers will need to make some type of change to adopt these habits. We know that for many people, this isn't easy.

Making changes, whether personally or within a business, takes courage and persistence. Although we may "know" that some type of change is needed, many of us are resistant to making that change.

This resistance often breaks down, however, when we realize that we are not operating the way we'd like and that there is a relatively easy means of operating better. That is the power of the Six Habits: They allow you to manage your organization more effectively and efficiently. Once you implement the Six Habits, you'll have more time to actually work on your business rather than in your business.

A final note concerns one of the lessons Mike uses to keep his employees focused on their goals. He calls this story "Don't Pick Up Nails."

The bright, shiny nails that are so frequently dropped by the carpenters on typical construction jobs are not useful. Picking them up is a distraction, a waste of time, and therefore a waste of money. The carpenters need to be framing the building, not picking up nails.

And so too do you need to be focused on the Six Habits. And too do you need to ignore the many bright and shiny distractions that come along every day.

CHAPTER 1

Set goals all the time

A True Story

One of our friends, and a former client, is Royal Robbins, a big rock-wall climber who achieved world fame in the 60s and 70s for his ability to go where no one had ever gone before. Royal was the first person to solo many of the biggest rock walls in this country and around the world, including the awesomely forbidding 3,000-foot sheer face of El Capitan, the famous granite monolith in Yosemite National Park.

Royal went on to found, run, and ultimately sell the outstanding outdoor apparel business that still carries his name. He continues to climb those forbidding rock walls, and he often gets the opportunity to tell his climbing and corporate stories to business and social organizations. (He's a big supporter of Rotary and the Boy Scouts of America.)

One of our favorite Royal Robbins stories concerns his solo climb on El Capitan. It illustrates the determination and the goal-focused attitude that this man drew upon to become the great climber he was, and still is.

During his solo ascent, Royal was a good part of the way up the face of El Capitan when his luck seemed to change. He already had gone farther than anyone previously had, but he had reached an apparent impasse. The barriers seemed overwhelming—the handholds were too small, the footholds too narrow, and the overhangs too imposing. He simply couldn't see a way to progress to the summit.

Royal stopped his efforts at this point and used his time to assess his situation. He figured that he had two real choices.

One was to simply retreat down the wall, and to make another attempt on another day. There certainly was no shame involved in this, because he already had done better than anyone previously had. He had a lot of fun in the process, and the wall would still be there for the next attempt.

The second choice, and the one that Royal took, was merely to see if he could go another 5 feet. He put the vision of achieving the summit out of his mind, and he focused only on the rock wall immediately in front of him.

Royal felt fairly confident that he could climb another 5 feet. And he reasoned that by doing so he certainly would make additional progress. Just as important, though, was the thought that he would have done his ultimate best; he would never question whether he might have gone just a little bit farther.

And this is the way that Royal Robbins became the first solo climber of El Capitan. He did it 5 feet at a time, resetting his goals as he achieved his last. He overcame obstacles that he didn't even know existed and other obstacles that, taken in total, seemed much too overwhelming to overcome.

And this became the way that Royal Robbins lived, and continues to live, his life. What a story.

COMPANY GOALS COME IN THREE FLAVORS

When Royal started to plan his journey to the top of El Capitan, he had a vision in his mind about the outcome of his adventure. He pictured himself, happy and excited, standing on top of the granite monolith, having just become the first to climb, alone, up the 3,000 vertical feet of this famous landmark.

Royal planned this climb very carefully and purposefully, and his vision was created from his desire to be the first to solo El Capitan, as well as from his knowledge of his own skills and determination. Nevertheless, it was a highly ambitious vision. After all, no one had ever done it.

Along the way, Royal quickly discovered that this was, indeed, not just a walk in the park. He wisely broke his climb into bite-sized chunks, setting goals to move just another 5 feet at a time. Thus, he moved toward his vision in 5 foot increments, which he could easily measure by looking back, as well as ahead, to see how far he had progressed.

Highly successful managers use a similar process. They create a clear vision of success for their group or organization, and they set incremental goals that move the group ever closer to that vision. And because everyone contributes in some way to the overall organization, these managers also ensure that everyone has individual goals that contribute to the achievement of the organization's goals.

Thus, we classify business-related goals into three types. All of them are interrelated as well as individually important in achieving success. Here they are:

- A long-term vision.
- Near-term goals.
- Goals for each individual.

Some guidance on vision

You've probably heard the word *vision* used in many ways, because there is no shortage of opinion on what it means. This creates great confusion among business owners and managers, which, in turn, often leads to total inaction. Why bother?

One of our favorite pieces of guidance on vision comes from *The Customer Driven Company*, by Richard Whiteley:

> *"[Vision is] a vivid picture of an ambitious, desirable future state that is connected to the customer and better in some important way than the current state."*

Highly successful managers know that this picture of an ambitious future state must include all of the stakeholders in the organization, including owners, employees, and customers. When all the stakeholders are included, they all contribute to achieving the vision.

For example, if the vision were merely to "maximize shareholder return," we should not be too surprised to find that many of the employees might be somewhat less than inspired. Although we might find a way to describe such a vision clearly, and to set an ambitious level of achievement, it likely would not represent a desirable condition to many employees.

People would not likely become excited about working tirelessly only for the benefit of the shareholders.

Similarly, if the vision were to exclude the customers, the company might forget about the continual actions it must take now and in the future. Financial success, after all, is measured as a past achievement—the company made $10 million last quarter. Customer success, on the other hand, is measured in the present and future—are we doing what we need to do to ensure that our customers are delighted and will continue to deal with us in the future?

Here's our guy, Mike, the founder and owner of a medium-sized construction company. He's talking about his company vision to a group of his professional friends.

Mike's Company

"Several years ago," said Mike, "I learned that my company should exist to serve me, and that I shouldn't be working to serve my company. This notion changed the way I thought. It motivated me to design a company that would meet my needs and wants, and not require me to spend unlimited hours as a slave to the company.

"One of my friends really brought it home when he said: 'Creating a vision for your company should be easy for you, Mike. You already visualize the completion of every customer's project before it leaves the drawing board. You just need to bring that thinking to your own business.'

"He was right! When I actually took the time to think about it, I could create in my mind the kind of company I'd like to have in the future. I decided to focus on my retirement from the firm—to fantasize about what my company would look like when I was ready to retire from it.

"So that's what I did, and it's what I continue to do. I created a company, in my mind, which:

- **Is better in some measurable way than it is now.**
- **Serves my customers in a significant way.**
- **Provides a great working environment for me and my employees.**

"One of my buddies pointed out that the Declaration of Independence is our country's vision. 'We hold these truths to be self-evident. That all men are created equal…' and so on. And our country progresses from year to year seeking to fulfill that vision. Sometimes we slip back, and sometimes we just get it wrong, but over time we work to fulfill that vision.

"It's the same with my company. Over time we work to fulfill the company vision. We don't always get it right, but we do make progress. Every year we get closer to what I imagined. And you can do the same thing, whether you own your own company or work as a manager. You just focus on your business whether it's a huge corporation or a small group."

We hope you'll take the time and thought to create your company vision. You'll be fashioning your long-term goal, thus challenging yourself to continually find ways to achieve that goal. We like the three areas of focus for your vision, identified previously, because they improve the situation of the major stakeholders in the company: owners, customers, and employees.

As Mike recognized, the company's vision is analogous to the U.S. Declaration of Independence, which represented the vision of our founding fathers. As with the Declaration, your vision should inspire people to do their best. It should energize them and provide them with true challenge and purpose. It should make each person feel that he or she can make a difference in your organization and perhaps the world. It becomes a rallying cry and an impetus to excellence.

A Client's Vision

One of our clients was a company that sold extruded metal products to the marine industry. They had recognized that they had no real unifying vision for the company.

Sure, people came to work every day knowing that they had to sell products at a profit. And many businesspeople would tell you that's all the vision they need.

But the owners of this company knew that they wanted more. They wanted a clear and simple "clarion call to action" that would compel everyone to achieve a level of success far beyond the current state of the company.

They considered many ideas. Why not be "the best in the industry," or "the leader in the region," or "the Nordstrom of the marine world"?

Although these ideas, and many others, were certainly grandiose and powerful-sounding, the owners and managers were not inspired by them. They considered them to be shop-worn and overused.

Bear in mind that you might not feel that way about a similar vision for your company. Being "the leader in the region" might inspire you and your team to great things. But it didn't do so for these owners.

In the end, the owners created a vision for their company that included statements about the treatment of employees, the focus on the customer, and the attitude that would propel them to financial success. The vision also included a statement that the firm intended to have "a company product on every U.S.-made boat."

When the owners and managers talked about this new statement, they began to consider its implications. Could they really do this? They didn't have accounts with every U.S. boat maker; how could they hope to fulfill a vision like this? Didn't it make more sense to just focus on the big players and sell lots of stuff to the big boys? Maybe they should rethink this new vision.

After some discussion, they concluded that their vision should compel the firm to create a broad reach into the market and to create national name awareness. They didn't need to have direct accounts with all boatmakers, nor did they need to sell only to large accounts.

They did, however, need to have a strategy for accomplishing this vision, in the near term and in the longer term. And that's what they focused on creating.

It certainly made sense to focus attention on big accounts—after all, they were big accounts for a reason. And the company had no intention of providing these customers with anything but the very best service, supplied directly by company employees.

But the team also considered how to gain access to all U.S. boat builders, even the smaller ones. They could create a new sales force, sell through other distributors, sell over the Internet, use a rep force, and so forth.

It was this focused thought process that resulted in strategies designed to fulfill this vision. And this vision had everyone engaged and compelled to achieve it.

There are, of course, many businesspeople who believe that the process of creating a company vision is little more than an exercise for academics. After all, they say, we know what needs to be done, so we go in each day and do it.

Unfortunately, in far too many cases, "just doin' it" is a poor substitute for a strong vision. Most often, it is a rallying cry to continue to do things the way they always have.

Conversely, a strong vision should inspire you to great performance—a level of performance that will bring you closer to actually achieving the vision itself. It also should guide you in your daily activities to create and reinforce your company culture.

The vision also should guide you in making the right decisions. It should assist you in cutting through complex technical issues to do the things that truly add value for the customer. It should guide you during routine decision-making ("Is this the type of client relationship that will move us closer to our vision?") and during conflict.

In a now-classic example of corporate stewardship, Johnson and Johnson showed a strong vision, and a strong commitment to their customers and their values, during the Tylenol crisis in 1982. Although the arsenic-contaminated drug was the work of a madman, J&J acted quickly to pull all products from its retailers, hospitals, and distributors. The CEO immediately used the media to reassure the public of J&J's commitment to safety, and the company reintroduced the drug only after they had designed and tested new safety packaging.

Before the incident, Tylenol was the number-one-selling over-the-counter pain and headache remedy. The recall cost the company approximately $100 million. But the firm stood as a case study of responsible corporate stewardship, and public opinion remained very strong and market share was almost entirely regained within three years.

Contrast this with the actions of Audi during approximately the same period of time. Many owners complained that the automatic transmissions of their Audi automobiles inadvertently shifted into reverse. Dozens of incidents were reported, many of them involving damage or injury. Audi responded by citing data to "prove" that their customers were not driving correctly. In effect, Audi denied any wrongdoing and specifically explained how drivers could cause the condition to occur by not operating the vehicle as Audi would have them operate it. Audi owners, as well as observers on the sideline, were offended by this position, and Audi sales declined sharply. They remained depressed for many years. (Audi worked very hard for many years afterward to change buyers' perceptions, and, at great cost, Audi is once again a respected brand in the United States.)

So what was the difference? It was a strong vision. J&J has a long-standing statement, called The Credo, which encompasses the company's vision. The first sentence states, "We believe our first responsibility is to the doctors, nurses and patients, to mothers and fathers and all others who use our products and services." And they proved it!

Creating your vision

A strong vision for your company fosters independent action, wisdom, empowerment, and willingness to take risks to do the right things. In our experience, virtually all employees embrace a clear vision as a guide in managing their own actions in a manner consistent with the company's vision. And we know that when people understand their goals, their performance and the performance of the organization improve.

Oftentimes, however, the company vision is dead on arrival because we balk at the process of creating and communicating it. Many managers and owners believe that creating a vision often seems to involve a whole lot of work. And you're awfully busy here, and you pretty much know what to do, and you've been doing it just fine for 11 years, so what's the point of taking time to do this?

We've also learned from business owners and managers that many of them believe that crafting a vision is highly time-consuming and may require special outside expertise. Additionally, they conclude that the finished product will be framed, hung in the hallway, and forever forgotten.

This self-directed conversation bludgeons them into inaction. This is curious, because virtually every manager we've known has remarked on the need for better communication, and virtually every business owner we've known has admitted that the business would improve if everyone knew where the company was going and could help push it in that direction.

How can we overcome this inertia? How can we begin to craft something like a vision, when we are faced with the perception of an energy wall that stops us in our tracks?

To overcome this perceived barrier, we can simplify the process. We like the vision to be a straightforward and heartfelt expression of the owner. Sure, you can hire someone to craft some elegant prose for you, but much will be lost if it doesn't express your true thoughts.

So, go back to that piece of guidance we gave you earlier about what a vision is.

> " *[Vision is] a vivid picture of an ambitious, desirable future state that is connected to the customer and better in some important way than the current state.*"

With this as basic guidance, you can create words or phrases that represent your vision. It's not necessary to craft elegant prose. Simply expressing the ideas in "bullet form" or as separate words or phrases is powerful and immediate, and can carry the flavor you want to convey to everyone. In fact, the more the vision sounds like your words, the better. Just make a start, even if that's just a few words, and you'll likely find that you can add to those words as time progresses.

The next step is to take all this to heart. And that requires frequent use and consistency of message. In your conversations with others, you must use the words in your vision as guidelines to your actions and the actions of everyone in the company.

————————A Client's Story————————

One of our clients had a vision that included the phrase "...and we will exhibit excellence in everything we do." Now, those of us outside the company might debate whether this is realistic, or achievable, or too idealistic, but the firm's owners were clear that this was part of their vision.

In the next few months, the company produced a detailed and comprehensive catalog that described all of its products, a first in the history of the firm. In the enthusiasm to complete the catalog, however, the company had committed several mistakes that were soon discovered by the sales force.

The owners discussed the issue and concluded that they had three alternatives. One, they could simply use the completed catalog and train the sales force to work around the mistakes. After all, it would cost tens of thousands of dollars to produce a new catalog, and the one they had was more than 99-percent accurate. Two, they could issue an errata page, a sheet that pointed out and corrected the mistakes, and include it with the catalog or send it to those who already had the catalog. This would be simple to implement and inexpensive, and wouldn't require sales force training. Third, they could redo the entire catalog.

The owners considered their vision during this discussion, and they concluded that they really had only one choice. They had to redo the catalog. And they did. It sent a powerful message throughout the organization—a message that said the owners were serious about their vision and that they were willing to pay real money to ensure that it was realized.

Near-term goals

When Royal Robbins was tempted to give up on his audacious first solo ascent on El Capitan, he reasoned that he might instead go just a few more feet. He put aside the notion of achieving the summit and instead focused on what he could accomplish right now.

So, he set a near-term goal for himself—one that he could focus on intently, but also one that was directly related to his vision of standing on the summit. Thus, he set his goals in bite-sized chunks (just go another 5 feet!). And immediately after he achieved that goal, he set a new one (to go the next 5 feet).

This is what successful business owners do all the time. They create bite-sized goals, which are directly related to fulfilling their vision, and they set new goals as soon as they achieve the old.

There are six characteristics for effective company goals. Company goals should be:

1. Directly related to fulfilling the company vision.
2. Challenging.
3. Reasonable.
4. Measurable.
5. No more than three in total.
6. Established at least yearly (and preferably more often).

Directly related to fulfilling the company vision

When your near-term goals are directly related to the company vision, you establish a standard of achievement that directs your daily ongoing efforts in the right direction: toward achieving your vision. For example, consider again the client who intended "to have a company product on every boat made in America." This portion of the company's vision compelled the company to create near-term (one- to two-year) goals, such as desired results for rep or distribution agreements, that would move the firm closer to that vision.

Challenging yet reasonable

We've found that almost all employees like to achieve goals, and we are highly in favor of truly challenging goals. We love to see companies achieve goals that they hadn't even imagined.

But the challenge needs to be within reason. If the goals are too easy, employees will be insulted, and they'll believe that we're patronizing them, or treating them as children. Conversely, if the goals are impossible, employees may give up before beginning. They'll be demoralized by a goal that only a delusional manager could embrace.

Measurable

If you measure your achievements regularly, you can manage your efforts effectively and take corrective actions as appropriate. This seems to be one of those obvious truisms that often is simply ignored. We've had far too many clients that did not measure their performance on a regular basis. Sure, they worked very hard every day, doing what they thought they should. And at the end of the month or the end of the year, they hoped that everything would be okay. We want them to do much better than okay, so we want them to measure all the time and take corrective actions immediately.

No more than three

We know from experience that having more than three goals at a time often overwhelms us. In many cases, the goals are so numerous as to become invisible.

And we know that the company goals should provide guidance to everyone in the company about the actions they should take every day. Everyone should be working every day to achieve the company goals. They can do this only when the goals are crystal clear.

--------- **A Client Story** ---------

One of our clients was a well-regarded surveying company in Canada. They were loaded with technical talent, and they were strong analytical thinkers.

When we first engaged with this company, we wanted to know something about the way that they operated. We asked lots of questions and listened carefully. When it came to the company's goals, this is how it went.

"So, it appears that you're all working hard to create a great company. Terrific. Now tell us about the company's goals. Let's start with this: Does the company have goals?"

"We sure do," said the CEO proudly.

"That's great to hear. Please, tell us what the goals are so that we can understand what you feel are your keys to success."

"Well," said the CEO, "I'll have to look them up for you. We have 17 goals, and I can never remember them all."

There it was. They had so many goals they couldn't remember them. They had to look them up. Not even the CEO knew the goals! We wondered how often the average employee looked up the company goals to guide her in her daily activities. Never?

So, we try to stick to no more than three over-arching goals. These are goals that encompass many smaller things—things that may at first seem to be goals in themselves, but really are the means for achieving the goals.

For example, you might at first choose to have separate goals for your revenues, gross profits, overhead expenses, and net profits. We've certainly witnessed plenty of companies that did just that. But in most cases, the overarching goal is net profit—you can't achieve the desired net profit without controlling the revenues, gross profits, and overhead.

To test this assumption, you might ask yourself a question such as this: If I missed my revenue goal, but still achieved my net profit goal (for example, by keeping expenses low), would I be satisfied? Would that be okay? If you answer yes, that's indicative that net profit is an overarching goal for you. As long as you achieve your net profit goal, you're happy. Revenues don't have to hit the target level, as long as you can manage the expenses to reach the desired net profit.

Conversely, if you answer no to the question, that indicates that revenues hold some high importance to your company and that achieving the stated net profit is not enough. This might occur, for example, if you are trying to capture market share—perhaps by lowering your prices to entice your competitors' customers to buy from you instead. In such a case, your goal might be a specific revenue number, or perhaps you'd have goals for both revenues and net profit.

Established at least yearly

Finally, we urge you to establish your near-term goals at least yearly. In fact, many successful managers establish monthly goals and then "roll them up" into yearly goals. So, in any given month, you'll know where you should be, and you'll always be planning ahead by at least a year, regardless of your fiscal calendar. You'll always be setting new goals.

Examples

Here are some examples, by no means meant to be comprehensive, to illustrate the nature of "goals," however well-intentioned, that do not meet the previous criteria. Our experience indicates that many stated goals sound quite good, but that they often don't function well as measuring sticks for success. So, we need to turn good intentions into solid, unambiguous goals.

INADEQUATE GOAL	Why It's Not a Good Goal	One Means to Make it a Good Goal
"IMPROVE CUSTOMER SERVICE"	This sounds fine, but it lacks a means of measurement.	"Achieve at least 80% on our quarterly customer-service survey"
"CUT OUR EXPENSES"	This is a noble endeavor, but it is a tactic in accomplishing the real goal.	"Achieve a net profit of 8%"
"SEND OUT A CUSTOMER SURVEY"	Sending out the survey is a poor goal, when results are what is needed.	"Achieve a score of 85% on our quarterly customer survey"
"TREAT OUR EMPLOYEES BETTER"	This is a nice idea that lacks a measurement.	"Attain a score of 90% on our quarterly employee survey"
"IMPROVE OUR CASH FLOW"	This lacks specificity and a means of measurement.	"Reduce our inventory by $200,000 by year end while maintaining our current fulfillment rates"
"PROVIDE TRAINING TO OUR EMPLOYEES"	This lacks a measurement.	"Each employee to attain a passing score on two company-approved training courses per year"

So where do you start? How do you decide what your goals should be? After all, there are virtually limitless possibilities here, because every business is different and because conditions change constantly. You can't just "steal" the goals from the business across the street; you need your own goals.

First, remember that one characteristic of a good company goal is that it be related directly to fulfilling the company vision. Second, you want the goals to be over-arching. They should include the achievement of many smaller objectives. If you combine these two notions, you'll be halfway home in creating goals for your company. You want to create over-arching goals that are related directly to fulfilling your company vision.

Oftentimes, we find that the appropriate goals for many companies fall into these three categories:

1. The financial health of the company.
2. The customer.
3. Some strategic initiative.

Financial health goal

For example, to measure the financial health of the company, we are indeed big fans of using net profit as a goal. In order to achieve a desired net profit, everyone in the company can take some role in contributing to increasing the revenues or decreasing the expenses that consequently result in the company's "bottom line." In this case, the company is like the fabled Golden Goose. The Golden Goose produced golden eggs only when she was healthy. So too must everyone contribute to the health of the company in order for the desired net profit to be produced.

There are plenty of alternative choices, of course, for a financial measure for your company goal for the current time period. We spoke about the possibility of using revenues as your goal when capturing market share. Depending upon the nature of your business, you might choose to focus on some specific line of the income statement, such as the gross profit or the overhead expenses. Alternatively, you might want to focus on the balance sheet, and look to generate higher cash flow by better management of your inventory or accounts receivable.

—————————————A Client's Story———————————————

One of our clients was a manufacturer of machinery used in the pulp and paper industry. They served clients all over the world, often in remote locations that lacked the modern conveniences that we take for granted.

The managers of the business were highly skilled and experienced. They knew how to determine what their clients needed, and they knew how to design, manufacture, and install the equipment that would meet those needs. They were true pros, and they worked hard every day to keep their business growing.

In their zeal to grow the business, however, they had taken their eye off the ongoing need to generate cash flow. More specifically, they had accumulated excessive inventory, and their customers were taking too long to pay them.

As a result, their cash was tied up in the goods sitting on the warehouse floor and in the goods and services they delivered to their customers, who hadn't yet paid them. They were moving at a fast rate, but the cash wasn't coming home.

Consequently, in their quarterly goal-setting exercise, the managers agreed to both inventory and accounts receivable goals, in addition to their normal net profit goals. And these goals were tied directly to the managers' performance rewards.

You can probably see where this is going. Once they were focused on these new goals, the managers made great progress at improving cash flow by reducing inventory and accounts receivable.

And the company owner smiled happily while he wrote the reward checks.

———

Whether you choose goals such as these or not, we advise you to choose goals that are affected by as many people in your organization as possible. You want to create an environment that allows everyone to contribute to achieving the goal.

For example, companies frequently establish a sales, or revenue, goal for the coming year. After all, all businesses want to grow, and this makes logical sense. Unfortunately, not everyone in the company can influence the desired sales level, or can be convinced that their involvement actually matters in moving the sales needle.

That's why we like to see the company goals related to net profits. Virtually everyone can contribute to the profitability of the company.

Customer-related goal

Whereas the net profit goal speaks to the financial health of the company in the near term, your customers determine your health in the longer term. It is very possible, and continually demonstrated by companies no longer around, that a company could generate strong profits this year while also alienating its customers, thus killing the Golden Goose.

Consequently, you might consider some type of survey to determine what your customers think about your company. Ultimately, you'd like to know if they'll buy from you at all, if they'll continue to buy from you, and what you have to do to ensure that they do.

Unfortunately, we don't know of the perfect survey for every company. After all, there are great differences in the nature of the work, the characteristics of the customers, the make-up of the staff, and so forth.

We've seen surveys that include virtually dozens of questions, from the way the receptionist treats the walk-in customer to the way that the bill is handled by the accounting department. All of these surveys are designed, in some way, to collect information that the company believes is somehow helpful.

Our guidance here is twofold. First, try to make the survey as short as possible. Focus on the things that are of paramount importance, and ignore low-value questions. Most folks simply don't enjoy filling out long questionnaires, or any questionnaires. Second, try to formulate over-arching questions—questions that include numerous other topics.

For example, there is a popular movement now to use only a single question in a customer survey. The question is "Would you recommend us to a friend?"

The logic here is that the customers' recommendations are of paramount importance. If the customer would recommend you, even though the receptionist may have been a little curt, you must be doing the important things right.

What we know here is that we like questions like this. It is overarching in its nature and focuses directly on what the customer thinks about your company.

Strategic goal

The goals for financial health and the customer are two of our favorites. They are effective and appropriate, most of the time, for many companies. And sometimes, these two goals may be all that you need. That's fine.

In other cases, a third goal may also be effective and appropriate. You will need to decide if this is the case for you, and create the correct goal (for example, perhaps a goal for inventory).

One of our favorite third goals is one that is related to some strategic issue. This is something that might be of high long-term value, is the focus of a critical issue, and would be important enough to nurture and manage.

Strategic goals might be called for when there are significant changes in the

- **Marketplace.**
- **Company's capabilities.**
- **Competitive environment.**
- **Company's opportunities.**

Marketplace changes might include new industry-wide trends, regulations that affect your business, technologies that affect your business, or other such factors common to your markets as a whole. For example, readers of daily news information are increasingly turning to the Internet and turning away from local newspapers. This industry-wide trend not only is causing the decline in newspaper readership, it also is leading to declining business for those who recycle newspapers, as well as for those who bundle and transport newspapers to the recycler.

Changes in the company's capabilities might result from the gain or loss of particularly skilled individuals, development of a new technology or capability, inability to borrow, or some other internal factor that might change the firm's ability to serve its markets. For example, fast-growing firms commonly acquire inventory and accounts receivables faster than they receive payments from customers. This leads to a decline in cash flow and a real restriction in the ability to continue to grow.

Changes in the competitive environment might include the emergence of a new direct competitor, increasing pressure from the company's suppliers, an inability to acquire enough skilled workers, or even a substitute product for the one you sell. For example, a local supermarket might offer a line of prepared dinner entrees for customers to take home, substituting this for the dinner that the customer might have bought at your restaurant.

Changes in the company's opportunities might include a newly identified type of customer, a halt to the fast-expanding business of your best customer, or a new ability to work with another firm to gain business together. For example, a high-end builder might team with an architect to acquire new business.

In each of these cases, you might decide to create a goal in order to exploit an opportunity or capability or to counter a threat or deficiency. For example, if the company's vision is to become a national player, establishing the first satellite office might be of sufficient strategic value to warrant a separate strategic goal, perhaps to include a number for net profit or customer growth.

Individual goals

Once you've created the company's near-term goals, you need to use your resources efficiently to attain them. A key means of doing this is to ensure that each individual has goals that relate to your company goals. Here's Mike again, talking about just that with one of his new employees.

───────────────── **Mike's Company** ─────────────────

"You can see now that I have a vision for the company, and that my vision drives the creation of our near-term goals and the goals for everyone on the team. We have goals for the year, for the quarter, sometimes even for the week. Here's what this looks like in a simple diagram.

Owners' Vision Drives the Goals

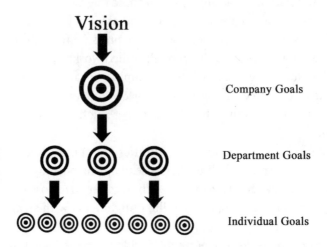

Vision

Company Goals

Department Goals

Individual Goals

"It looks simple on paper, but we put lots of thought into all the activities represented by that little drawing. For example, one of the items in my vision is to have a company that encourages all employees to take as much responsibility as they can handle. I want employees who always push me and push each other to excel. And I want them to lead, not follow, whenever they can.

"Our annual goals, on the other hand, are more closely focused. They usually pertain to a specific level of performance for the coming year. Next year, for example, we want to make 8 percent net profit. This is one of our company goals, and everybody is focused on achieving it.

"Individual goals are owned by each employee. Everybody has goals that they establish with the help of their supervisor. Every employee finds this out when they work with their supervisor. And those goals must help the company reach its overall goals. We want all the sled dogs to pull in the same direction.

"Let me show you how we do this. Let's go back to that item in my vision that I described to you—the one where I want all the employees to take as much responsibility as possible.

"One of our employees is a very talented new manager. But he has never had responsibility beyond his current level. We think that he can go way beyond his current level, and we want to help him. So, one of his personal goals by year end is to create and implement a training program for all supervisors, the managerial level that reports to him. We believe that by creating this program he will actually grow faster as a manager, because he'll need to know the information extremely well in order to teach it to others. Creating the course will also improve his organizational and presentation skills."

As an excellent manager himself, Mike will work frequently with this new manager to ensure that he achieves his goals. Mike may only need to touch base with the manager for limited time each week, but his interactions will ensure that the manager's actions are well directed and executed. We'll talk more about these weekly "one-on-one" meetings in a later section; they're an important factor in the success of a company such as Mike's.

Now we can look at these goals from the other direction. When we add up everyone's individual goals, they should achieve the company goals. And the company goals should move the company closer to the owner's vision.

In a diagram, all the individual goals add first to the department or business unit goals, which collectively then add to the company goal. Achieving the company goal, created for perhaps only the current fiscal year, moves the company closer to the company vision. It looks like this:

Goals Move the Organization Toward the Vision

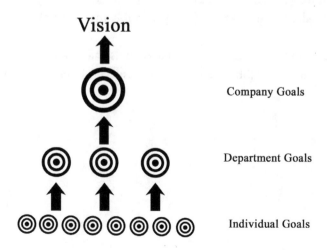

Vision

Company Goals

Department Goals

Individual Goals

Here's another way to think about all this. Imagine that you had a goal to place a heavy monument on top of a mountain. You knew that if you got all of your friends together to help that you could achieve this vision. But there wouldn't be any place for slackers. Nobody could just look busy while not directly helping.

You might consider several ways to accomplish this. For example, you might build a road up to the top of the mountain and truck the monument to the top. Alternatively, you might merely clear a path, put the monument on a sledge, and pull it up by brute force. Finally, you might somehow acquire a helicopter, train someone to fly it, and airlift the monument to the top.

Regardless of which of these three strategies you chose, everyone in the group would have a specific position, with specific individual goals, to get the monument to the top. When everyone performed their role successfully, the overall goal would be achieved. Simple, huh?

As with the company goals, there should be clear criteria for establishing individual goals. Here they are (looking suspiciously like the criteria for company goals):

- **Directly related to fulfilling the Company Goals.**
- **Challenging.**
- **Reasonable.**
- **Measurable.**
- **No more than three in total.**
- **Established at least yearly (and preferably more often).**

Here are some examples of individual goals that do not meet the criteria. Once again, our job here is to turn these well-intentioned thoughts into solid unambiguous goals.

INADEQUATE GOAL	Why It's Not a Good Goal	One Means To Make it a Good Goal
"Improve your customer service skills"	*This sounds fine, but it lacks a means of measurement.*	*"Achieve at least 80% on our quarterly customer-service survey."*
"Make a profit on projects you oversee"	*This lacks specificity (some projects or all projects or the average across all projects?) and measurement.*	*"Make a minimum 10% profit on every project you oversee."*
"Coordinate your activities with the Design Department"	*This lacks a measurement*	*"Attain 99.5% accuracy in fulfillment of requests from the Design Department."*
"Attend two trade shows this year"	*Mere attendance is a trivial (not challenging) standard for a goal.*	*"Produce a return on investment of 150% for all trade shows attended."*
"Take two training courses this year"	*Again, mere attendance is a trivial (not challenging) standard for a goal.*	*"Attain a passing score on two company-approved training courses this year."*

Let's return now to the goals and vision diagram, reproduced at the top of page 38. When you craft company and individual goals (and perhaps department goals) that are pointed to your vision and that are all in alignment, you ensure that everyone in your organization is doing the right things to move you in the right direction.

Goals Move the Organization Toward the Vision

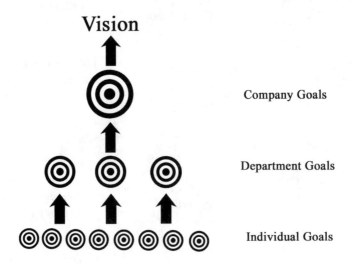

DON'T PICK UP NAILS

―――――――――――― Mike's Company ――――――――――――

"**O**kay, Tony," says Roberto, Tony's supervisor, "let's take a walk around. I'll show you the project here, and then I'll get you started."

Roberto, who works directly for the owner, Mike, first introduces Tony to the other workers. There are eight of them working on this project. Then he takes Tony to the top floor of the building, where a couple of the guys are putting up the framing. They work quickly and efficiently, sawing lumber, leveling, and nailing.

As Tony walks along the future hallway of the building, he notices dozens of pristine nails scattered all over the floor of the sprawling construction site. They shimmer and sparkle like metallic gems. Stepping over them are several carpenters, all working intently.

Roberto notices Tony staring at the floor. "What's the matter, Tony?"

"It's these nails. Perfectly good nails all over the floor. Why don't the guys pick them up and use them, instead of just digging others out of their aprons? Isn't that kind of wasteful?"

Roberto smiles, not in a condescending way, but almost like he just found something valuable.

"Tony, you've just discovered one of the management principles that we live by in this company. We even have a phrase for it: Don't Pick Up Nails!

"That's what we tell all our workers and all our managers. We want everybody to focus on the *vital few* important things and to ignore the *trivial many* things that distract them.

"You're right, Tony. It does seem wasteful to have all those nails going unused. And we teach our carpenters some tricks so that they won't drop so many. But these carpenters are being paid a good salary, and they need to be efficient and productive in framing this building. Picking up nails is nothing but a distraction. It takes too long, and the nails are relatively inexpensive. If we paid these guys to pick up nails, we'd be losing money and productivity."

"Yeah," Tony says. "I can see the logic in that. But it still bothers me that all those good nails are just sitting there."

"That's the whole point, Tony. To us, they're no longer good nails. The good nails are in the carpenters' aprons.

"As you work here," Roberto continues, "you'll see that there are many things, like those nails, that can easily become distractions—things that can consume time and resources and divert us from our goals. It takes discipline to ignore these distractions. And unfortunately, lots of distractions seem to be as bright and shiny as those nails—they're real tough to ignore."

We've all had Tony's experience—instead of nails it's just something else that distracts us from our goals. We knew a manager who would interrupt any meeting, even a large, client-focused one, to leap out of his chair to answer his phone, without even knowing who might be calling him. And we'll guess that you've met folks who can easily be diverted by a knock on the door, or a phone call, or a text message to drop what they're doing in order to deal with the interruption, no matter how trivial.

These are well-intentioned folks, make no mistake, but they have let urgency substitute for importance. That ringing phone or insistent knock just begs for a response, but too many times they represent issues that simply should be ignored. They're nothing more than bright, shiny nails.

SAY NO TO THE HAMSTER WHEEL

You might have seen a hamster wheel. It's a small circular wire cage that rotates around a central axle, much like a tire rotates around the axle of your car, and inside the cage is an energetic hamster. In our usual image of the hamster, he is running furiously, spinning the wheel at high speed.

From the hamster's point of view, life inside the wheel may actually appear quite normal. The hamster is an energetic animal by nature, and he's doing what he knows how to do: run like heck. And he's making real progress, too; he can see the blur of spokes flying by him as he runs.

Unfortunately, his position relative to the ground beneath the cage indicates that he's actually going nowhere. He's really just expending lots of calories without creating real forward progress, although, as the line goes, he's making great time.

A Client's Story

Early in our engagement with a new client, we discovered a beehive of activity. People and equipment were in constant motion. It was, at first, quite an impressive display. The place was hopping.

The company was a manufacturer of highly specialized communications equipment. In fact, at the time, they were the only provider of this equipment in the country, having pioneered the products and virtually created the market space themselves. It was a highly creative place, and we really liked the owners and employees.

Unfortunately, it also was a place of wasted motion. People were, literally and figuratively, running in circles. Goals were either missing or unclear, people's assignments and responsibilities were undefined or ambiguous, and there were more than a few squabbles about who should be doing what. But, boy, everybody sure was busy, and it certainly typified the type of environment common in many high-growth startup companies.

We could picture these humans in their own hamster wheels. They were spinning round and round, but they weren't making progress toward any ambitious goals. In fact, there were no goals for the company or the individuals.

All too often, the hamster cage is a metaphor for managers. They, too, run hard, expending lots of calories. Instead of a wheel-shaped cage, though, they move people and resources. And they often feel satisfied that this constant hard work is some form of progress. After all, they can see the spokes flying by them—things are moving.

Real progress, of course, is the movement of the individual and the company relative to their goals. If they can find a way to look outside their cage, they can determine if they are making real progress or simply spinning their wheels.

Establishing goals regularly, and measuring progress relative to those goals, allows you to see outside the cage. It provides you with a big-picture focus on the *vital few*, and it substitutes focus and direction, toward a clear and desired outcome, for frantic activity.

Say no to the hamster wheel. Have clear goals for everyone, establish them regularly, and measure progress relative to those goals all the time.

Points to Remember

- Establish a clear vision for the company (a very long-term goal).
- Create annual, or more frequent, goals for the company that:
    - Are directly related to fulfilling the company vision.
    - Are challenging.
    - Are reasonable.
    - Are measurable.
    - Do not exceed three at a time.
- Agree on annual, or more frequent, goals for everyone that:
    - Are directly related to fulfilling the company goal.
    - Are challenging.
    - Are reasonable.
    - Are measurable.
    - Do not exceed three at a time.
- Ensure that everyone's individual goals will collectively achieve the company goals.
- Make goal-setting a regular habit in the company. Do it today, and keep doing it regularly.

- Don't pick up nails: Identify the distractions in your business—the bright, shiny nails on the floor—and determine how you'll ignore those distractions and focus everyone on their goals.
- Say no to the hamster wheel. Ensure that you're moving toward your goals, not just moving around at high speed.

CHAPTER 2

Focus on the process, not a plan

---— A True Story ——---

One of us is a pilot, and some of our best friends are even pilots. One of the things we all have in common is our love for a planning process. And it's the process itself, more than the actual plan, that is most compelling.

In training to become a pilot, there are many technical challenges to master. You must be able to forecast the weather, read an aviation map, navigate using electronic aids, and master the plane's controls—all in an environment of moving air, changing weather, and other nearby airplanes.

Perhaps most important, however, is the ability to fly and land safely when something goes wrong. Your life and the lives of others depend upon it.

Consequently, a pilot spends many hours practicing maneuvers that are designed to respond to emergencies or changes in pre-arranged plans. The goal is to provide the pilot with the skills to adjust quickly and correctly to these situations—to allow him to make new plans when the old ones are obsolete. In effect, a pilot is trained to make rapid and effective changes to the careful plans that he previously created.

For example, on one of our flights, we had an apparent fire in the instrument panel when we were thousands of feet above the ground. A thin haze first started to seep out of the panel, followed by an increasingly heavy flow of acrid-smelling smoke.

This was no joke, and it required a quick response. We couldn't simply pull off to the side of the road or roll down the window and call AAA. It was all up to us.

We had been trained well, however, and it was the training that we received in the process of planning that allowed us to respond correctly.

We needed a new plan—a new sequence of actions that would land us safely. After all, our original plan didn't include an electrical fire at 4,000 feet!

Because of our training, we knew that there was a logical exit from this situation, and we approached the task with a heightened sense of awareness. A fire of any kind in an airplane is not a preferred activity, so we needed to tackle this quickly and effectively.

First, we methodically shut down the airplane's electrical system, including our instruments and radios. Though this may seem counter-intuitive, the distinctive acrid smell of the smoke indicated that the fire was electrical in nature, so turning off the electrical system was the logical means of attempting to terminate the fire.

Next, we confirmed our position and located some alternative locations to make a landing. We looked constantly for nearby air traffic, and we were especially diligent about our maneuvers because we no longer had radio contact with any unseen planes or ground control personnel.

Finally, we spotted a small airfield nearby, with minimal air traffic in the area, where we were able to land the plane safely. With a sigh of relief, we walked away to recount our actions and discuss what we had done and might have done better.

Overall, we did okay because our instructors had provided us with a planning process. In the face of unforeseen circumstances, we knew how to adapt and respond. We were able to discard our old plans and quickly adapt to our new situation.

And with a little luck, we'll never do this again.

MOST BUSINESSES DON'T HAVE A PLAN

Through the years, we've spoken to hundreds of business owners about their business plans and their planning processes. More specifically, we've asked them individually and we've polled them as a group at our seminars to determine if they have a business plan of any kind and how they use it.

Initially, we expected that a fair number of them would tell us that they had some type of business plan and that they followed that plan throughout the year. Boy, were we wrong.

Approximately one in 20 business owners told us that they had a business plan of any kind. At first, we thought that this low number somehow might be due to the particular attendees of our seminars. Somehow, perhaps, we were getting the "non-planners." Maybe they were attending our seminars because they didn't have a plan and they were smart enough to know that they needed help. We didn't really know the answer, but that was our theory.

Over time, however, that one-in-20 number has been quite consistent, regardless of attendance at seminars. Only about 5 percent of the independently owned businesses that we've encountered created a business plan of any kind.

And of that one in 20, many fewer actually use the business plan as a tool for ongoing management. They have a plan, but it seems to sit on the shelf until next year, or the year after, when the company makes a new plan. Essentially, the plan is generally ignored throughout the year; there is little effort to direct day-to-day actions based upon its strategies or goals, which go largely forgotten.

An even smaller percentage of owners provide rewards to their employees when the goals of the plan are met. There is, in effect, no link between the stated goals of the company and the rewards given to employees who help achieve those goals.

Why so few? Why do so few owners have a plan, let alone a planning process?

Some business owners say that having a business plan is useless because things change so quickly. By the time they create a plan, they say, it's already obsolete. Why bother?

Other owners say that they don't have the time to do a fancy plan that only an MBA would like. After all, they've got a business to run. Let the MBAs stay at home with their calculators and expensive mechanical pencils—at least they'll be out of the firing line of running a real business.

Other owners say that they don't do a business plan because they don't know how, or they function better as a crisis manager, or they tried it once and it didn't work. There are numerous other reasons as well.

All of these owners have one thing in common: Creating a business plan doesn't appear to offer more value to them than continuing to do what they're already doing. They simply haven't been convinced that making a plan is worth their time and effort.

We believe that the reason for this is not obvious. Business owners have been taught incorrectly that the plan itself is the article of value.

Conversely, we believe that the *process* of planning is much more important that the plan itself. The plan is merely the logical outcome of an effective ongoing planning process, and it's the planning process that allows businesses to act nimbly and effectively in the face of change.

Let's look at this a bit closer. Many owners and managers have been led to believe that they should create a plan, stick rigorously to their plan, and then expect success to knock on their door. If this were the case, of course, all business owners and managers would create a business plan in their first week on the job. Only a fool would ignore a sure thing, and business owners and managers certainly are not fools.

This myth is further enhanced by pithy and attractive metaphors that often are used to teach us about the value of having a business plan. One of our personal favorites refers to the sport of scuba diving, where responsible divers plan the depth, time, and location of each dive well before they enter the water. This planning is essential in scuba diving. If you do something wrong, such as stay at great depth for too long and then surface too quickly, you could die. So, to impress business owners about the urgency and importance of creating a business plan, coaches and authors take a page from the scuba divers' training book and tell the owners to "plan your dive, and dive your plan."

This seems like logical and efficient advice. Make a plan and stick to it. It even has overtones of the early childhood urgings from our mothers. "Just stick to it, kid, and you'll come out okay." This is powerful stuff indeed.

THE PROCESS IS MORE IMPORTANT THAN THE PLAN

Unfortunately for business owners and managers, this advice is not for them. The true value of creating a business plan is the **process** of creating it. The plan itself is of much less value. This is what business owners haven't been taught (and it's not their fault: No one taught them!).

Dwight Eisenhower, the 34th president of the United States, was a true advocate of this concept, and he certainly knew a thing or two about planning. Previous to becoming the 34th president of the United States, he was a very-rare five-star general in the Army and the Supreme Commander, Allied Forces in Europe during World War II. He famously stated: "In preparing for battle I have always found that plans are useless, but planning is indispensable." Or, as a recent officer at West Point stated, "No plan survives contact with the enemy."

Eisenhower knew that the best of his plans could quickly become obsolete under the fast changing conditions of a battlefield. He needed a high-level *ability* to plan in order to stay ahead of the enemy's maneuvers.

So how does all of this translate to your business? What do we mean when we say that the planning process is more important than the plan itself?

We've often had many business owners rail against the creation of a business plan by telling us that their industry, competitors, or opportunities are simply moving too fast. By the time they would write a business plan, they say, the conditions will have changed so drastically that the plan will be useless. If only they were in a stable and predictable environment, then it would make more sense to have a plan.

Interestingly, there is some truth to their observation. When conditions are stable, it's relatively easy to adhere to a plan. Unfortunately, such conditions rarely exist. How often have conditions been stable in your organization and industry for any real length of time?

When conditions are unstable, however, the planning process is of much greater value than a specific plan. Let's look at another common metaphor for business to see why.

Business owners often are told that creating a business plan is analogous to making a plan for a long sailing adventure. Before setting sail, the captain should make a plan. He needs to predict the expected sea and weather conditions to outfit the boat properly, plan daily progress, and measure and monitor that progress. So, too, say many sage advisors, should business owners "chart their course."

Let's look at two different scenarios to test the value of those pre-trip preparations. We'll consider first a condition of great weather and no troubles, and then we'll consider a condition of great turmoil and constant upset.

A Trip in Calm Seas

For the boat captain in calm seas and beautiful weather, there is little concern about fulfilling his pre-cruise plan. He can meander wherever he chooses, take side trips and detours, and even kick back and loaf, and he'll still get to his destination.

In effect, he can choose any number of destinations, and he'll always get there safely and uneventfully. He'll appear to be a planning genius, and his passengers will be thrilled by the predictability of the trip—they'll get to see all the things they were promised in the colorful fold-out brochure.

A Trip in a Storm

For the boat captain in tumultuous conditions, things are considerably different. After only a short time on the water, nothing goes according to "plan." The seas are unexpectedly heavy and the weather has deteriorated. The boat is in the middle of a potentially disastrous situation. Depending upon the planning skills and sailing skills of the captain, there are a couple of possible outcomes.

First, let's assume that the captain either had not created a plan at all before beginning the trip or that he had simply created a fair-weather plan—a plan that didn't take much thought and merely relied upon good conditions. He didn't plan for bad weather and rough seas, and now he has to figure out a solution. While trying to keep his footing on a shifting slippery deck, while trying to direct passengers to help him (he didn't bring along a seasoned crew because he didn't plan for these conditions), and while attempting to determine his position and heading, he simultaneously attempts to determine how to save his boat and passengers. This is not a fun day.

Alternatively, let's assume that the captain not only created a plan before leaving the dock, but that he used an effective planning process to do so. He used a methodical and proven process to assess the likely situations that he might encounter, and he determined his courses of action for each of these situations. He even took it a step further, and determined what he would do in various cases of emergency. He created logical steps to take in any given situation, distilling the many possibilities into a logical decision tree. Now that a crisis is upon him, the captain knows what to do and how best to do it. It will be a rough sail, but he'll make it home.

Okay, we admit that our story is a bit simplified. But we hope to convince you that a planning process is needed most when conditions are fluid (pun intended).

It is when conditions are ever-changing, not when they are predictable, that it is most important to have an excellent planning process. Such a process considers real-life conditions and adapts to those conditions constantly.

Conversely, it is when conditions don't change at all that following the same plan works best. We just don't know of any businesses where that occurs for any real length of time.

Take a look at your own organization for a moment. How many months in a row can you count in which there were no, or relatively few, changes in your own company or in the business environment in which you operate? How many months in a row has your business enjoyed calm seas and beautiful weather like our lucky sailor?

There are, of course, owners and managers who merely continue doing whatever they did yesterday or last month, regardless of any changes in their business environment. And they might actually be fortunate enough to succeed. But we suspect that you've got too much at stake in your organization to leave things to luck or good fortune.

CREATING A PLANNING PROCESS

So what do we mean by a planning process? Isn't that just a confusing way of saying that we're going to make a plan?

Here's how we think of it: The planning process is an organized manner for obtaining interrelated information to create an effective plan. A key word here is *organized*. An effective planning process relies on an organized manner of collecting and analyzing all relevant information, and a good plan is the product of this effort.

We're going to give you some guidance on building a planning process, but first we want to give you some examples. This will illustrate the value of a process clearly, before you get into the details of creating an actual process for your company.

If you were a home builder, the process of building a home would be much more valuable to you than the ability to build only one particular type of building. For example, if you only knew how to build one floor plan, you'd only be able to build houses that were all identical. And you'd probably be confused when a homeowner wanted to make changes to that floor plan. You'd take too long to figure out how to implement the changes, and the cost to you and to the customer would be too high. And you certainly wouldn't be able to sell homes to people who didn't like your one and only model.

Conversely, if you understood the *process* of home building, you'd be able to make changes whenever required. And you'd do it efficiently. It would be cost-effective for the homeowner and profitable for you. You'd have great flexibility in your strategies. You'd be able to operate in a wide variety of neighborhoods, for numerous customers with widely varying preferences. You could build whatever the customer wanted, and you could do it quickly and profitably.

There are other examples all around us that illustrate the importance of a planning process. In many cases, the process is not only more important than any specific plan, it can mean the difference between success and failure. Or even life and death.

In a recent example of excellence in both emergency planning and airmanship, a commercial airliner in New York City survived a collision with a flock of large birds, shutting down the plane's powerful engines. The pilots were now commanding a huge glider full of passengers, and they had no attractive options.

But the pilots had been trained well. They quickly determined that they had two critical tasks to complete to ensure the safety of all on board.

First, they needed to find a place to put the airplane down—somewhere other than in the midst of the multi-story skyscrapers all around them. Because pilots are trained regularly to locate backup landing locations when emergencies arise, this activity was part of the planning process that the pilots had learned and practiced in their training sessions.

Second, they had to land the plane in such a way as to minimize damage. Here, too, the airlines train their pilots on the proper means of bringing down an airplane when the engines fail. It's not easy, but it can be done, and the pilots had practiced this repeatedly in elaborate and expensive simulators to hone their skills.

So, although the pilots likely had not practiced the specific situation they faced in New York, they had learned an effective process for planning. They knew how to assess the current situation, decide when alternative plans were required, and execute the precise maneuvers that had the best chance for the survival of everyone on board.

The pilots knew that they could not make it to any nearby airports; the plane was sinking too fast. But they saw a wide and relatively long flat surface that was within range and perhaps could substitute for a paved runway: the Hudson River. No one had ever filed a flight plan that included the phrase "and now land in the Hudson River," but that is exactly what the pilots decided to do.

Next, the pilots knew that they had to bring the plane down on the surface of the river, and do so in a way that would minimize damage. News commentators referred to this maneuver as a "water landing," which seems a bit contradictory, but why quibble?

The pilots knew that a water landing was a highly dangerous activity. The surface of the river would not behave as a concrete or asphalt runway, and the sudden drag of the plane in the water could quickly cause the plane to tilt, skid, or completely flip over.

But all that training in the process of planning paid off. Everyone walked, or swam, away safely.

There are other everyday examples where the planning process is more important that any specific plan. In football, the quarterback calls for a specific play when in the huddle, then assesses the field situation just before he runs his planned play, and then sometimes calls for a new plan just before the action starts. Military commanders perform similarly, calling for a change of tactics or strategy as new conditions unfold, thus abandoning the original plan. Even a good chef does the same, creating a different sauce or even an entirely new meal depending on the availability of ingredients or a mistake in the kitchen.

So, how do you do this in your business? How do you create a planning process—an organized manner for obtaining interrelated information to create an effective plan?

There are five fundamental steps for creating a planning process. Each of these steps is easy to understand; they just take some dedication to implement properly and regularly.

1. Identify the right information.
2. Engage everyone in collecting the information.
3. Create successful strategies.
4. Modify the strategies in light of new information.
5. Do this frequently.

Identify the right information

Let's go back to our sailboat captain, the one who knew how to plan, to find a useful analogy for identifying the right information for a business planning process. Our captain knew that before he took to the seas he should collect information about tides, weather, sea lanes, and crew availability. Only when he had all this interrelated information could he properly set his destination and the strategies to get there. And he used a robust planning process that allowed him to make effective changes to his plans when the conditions changed.

For any business, there likewise are types of information that owners should collect in order to set the right strategies and goals. The process of collecting this information, and then constructing these strategies and goals, will increase the probability of creating a successful business, as long as you do it on a regular basis.

We're going to show you two ways to conduct your planning process. One is the traditional approach and one is a more regular, frequent, and less time-consuming way that allows for quick changes and high flexibility. We think that both approaches are useful to you.

The traditional approach

We mentioned earlier that perhaps only one in 20 businesses have a plan. That still adds up to a large number of companies that conduct some type of planning activity.

In our experience, most of these companies engage in a plan-building activity that usually takes place once a year, at most. They usually do this sometime within the final three months of their fiscal year because they want the information to be up-to-date and relevant for the coming year. Some of them engage a wide variety of managers and employees, and take many days or even weeks to collect and analyze the desired information and to construct their final plan.

So what's wrong with all that? Actually, in our experience, this type of planning event has some strong benefits. For example, it's a good first step as a training ground for learning the process of planning, which is critical to the business. Additionally, many of these annual planning events collect the right types of information and conduct the planning activity in a thoughtful and logical way.

On the other hand, as countless managers have told us, this is the only time of the year that they "think about where the business is going." For the rest of the year, they work hard every day "to do the real work."

If there is a problem with this intense annual activity, then, it is with the infrequency of it. Conducting your planning activity once a year is simply not enough, and we'll talk about that when we discuss an alternative activity.

The traditional annual activity, however, does provide some training in both collecting the right information and in beginning to build a planning process. So we urge you to take advantage of that training value.

Following is a business plan outline that you can use for this training as well as for the actual analysis of information and the creation of your plan. Just as pilots use checklists to guide them in their activities, so, too, can you use this outline as your checklist to guide you in your planning activities. There are other useful and effective outlines you might use, but this one has served us well.

A Business Plan Outline

1. Purpose

2. Executive Summary

3. The Company
    A. Vision
    B. Mission statement
    C. History

       D. Current status

       E. Competitive advantages and disadvantages

4. Marketing Plan

       A. Market and industry analysis

       B. Market segments

       C. Competitive environment

       D. Positioning

       E. Key customers

       F. Market opportunities

       G. Target markets

       H. Goals and marketing strategies

       I. Resources needed and milestones

       J. Sales forecast

       K. Customer service

5. Operational Plan

       A. Operational goals and strategies

       B. Management team and organizational chart

       C. Implementation plans

       D. Risks

6. Legal and Professional Issues

7. Financial Plan

       A. Historical financial statements

       B. Pro formas

       C. Ratio analyses

       D. Sources and uses of funds

In Appendix B, based upon this outline, we've provided you with tools and details that will help you in your planning process and in creating your plan. This will give you a strong set of training materials for all involved.

You might guess, correctly, that collecting and analyzing the information for your plan is likely to be an intense and time-consuming activity. There's just a whole lot of stuff to do here. That's a major reason that companies use this traditional approach only once a year.

Additionally, this only-once-a-year approach is inherently inflexible. The plan that is created for today's situation often becomes obsolete as the year progresses. After all, things change constantly, both within the company and in the company's business environment. What worked yesterday may not work well today.

That's why you need to do something else. You need an efficient way to assess your situation regularly in order to adapt to fast-changing conditions.

An additional approach

And that's what compelled us to look for an additional approach—one that takes less time but still provides you with the tools you need to adapt quickly to changes in your business and your environment. The notion is not to replace the traditional approach, at least not immediately, but rather to add another tool to the planning process so that you can retain the training value of the traditional approach while greatly increasing adaptability. This builds and strengthens your planning process on a regular basis, making it a habit within your company, while providing the flexibility to change plans in the face of changing conditions.

We concluded that there are four major categories of information that allow you to make quick and effective decisions and to create winning strategies—strategies to achieve success—in the face of changing conditions. The information is focused both inward on the company's capabilities and outward on the company's business environment. You'll find details on each of these sections in Appendix B, but here they are:

- The strengths and deficiencies of your company.
- Industry forces—the favorable and unfavorable trends in your industry.
- Your competitive environment.
    - Direct rivals.
    - Imminent rivals.
    - Substitutes for your products or services.
    - Supplier pressure.
    - Customer pressure.
- Your opportunities.

At first glance, these four major categories sound a bit like the traditional SWOT analysis (strengths, weaknesses, opportunities, and threats). And they do share some similarities. For example, they both consider your company's internal strengths and weaknesses as well as its external opportunities and threats.

But we'll coach you to look a bit deeper than that. For example, the favorable and unfavorable trends in your marketplace may not be an immediate threat or opportunity, and so might be ignored in a traditional SWOT analysis.

Surprisingly, Kodak did this in the early days of digital photography, when, despite its own patents for digital imaging, it stuck too long with its traditional film business while other firms raced ahead in digital photography. Some of these firms had no real experience in traditional film photography, but they knew how to make pixels dance, and they outpaced the company whose name had been synonymous with photography for many years.

Decades before, the Swiss did something similar when they ignored the inexpensive (though exceedingly accurate) quartz watch movements being sold by the Japanese. The Swiss simply didn't see these cheap watches as a threat to their near-monopoly of high-end mechanical time pieces swathed in gold and jewels.

Similarly, a traditional SWOT analysis might not identify a threat or opportunity posed by an emerging change in a supplier relationship, because threats are most commonly viewed as actions taken by direct competitors and opportunities are most commonly viewed as movements in the marketplace. But a supplier can cause real joy or heartburn in a business.

For example, many manufacturing firms have long used suppliers that provide them with product components that arrive just in time (JIT), thus minimizing inventory costs. This requires a highly skilled supplier, but it can mean big savings for the manufacturer. So, when suppliers started to offer JIT inventory, savvy manufacturers seized it as a terrific opportunity. Those who didn't cited numerous reasons as to why it wouldn't work.

In effect, the four-category model here is meant to be a day-to-day assessment tool. Like the outline, it is a checklist (in this case a visual checklist), that reminds you of the key activities you must conduct to stay abreast of changing conditions. It compels you to think strategically on a regular basis, not just once in a while, and it allows you to create strategies that quickly adapt to your changing environment.

At this point, we'd coach you to ask yourself and your team this question on a regular basis, at least monthly:

"What has changed in these four categories?"

When you can answer that question quickly, accurately, and on a regular basis, you'll have taken the first important step to creating a robust and flexible planning process.

Engage everyone in collecting information _____

As we noted previously, most business plans are created at the end of the fiscal year, as a once-a-year activity. Typically, a great deal of energy and time is expended by the team to collect and analyze information, create strategies and goals, and write the plan—all in a short period of time.

This is a bit like preparing for a track meet by working out the week before the event. We'll have expended some effort, for sure, but our results are likely to be disappointing. Things might have been different, however, if a training regimen had been a regular part of our life style, rather than a last-minute rush.

So, how can we change this? How can you get everyone to value and participate in a planning process? How can you make it a part of your organization's culture?

Actually, the answer to these questions is almost too simple: You allow, encourage, and make it fun for everyone to participate in the process.

You allow it by opening yourself to the notion that, indeed, everyone can make a valuable contribution. After all, everyone (collectively) is smarter than one person (you).

You encourage it by coaching everyone on the four specific categories of information you seek and the ways in which they can help you collect it. The business plan outline and the tools we'll discuss will help you do this.

You make it fun by showing everyone the plans you create, describing how those plans flowed from the contributions they made in assisting you, and praising and rewarding them for those contributions. In other words, you provide a link between their efforts and the group's results.

―――――――――― A Client's Story ――――――――――

One of our clients was a supplier to the marine industry. They coached their salespeople to create strong relationships with their customers so that they could anticipate their customers' needs. They also coached their salespeople to provide their customers' feedback to the engineering and marketing groups in order to anticipate potential new products that might be developed. This process resulted in the invention of a new product for the industry that promised to lower the cost of boat manufacture while providing a superior appearance to the exterior.

―――――――――― A Client's Story ――――――――――

One of our clients was an architectural firm specializing in buildings for educational institutions. They trained their project managers to collect information, on a regular ongoing basis, from clients, vendors, and contractors that was useful in their planning process.

As a result, the firm was constantly receiving updated information on the competitive environment, trends in the industry, and emerging needs of the client. This provided the firm with some significant strategic advantages relative to its competitors, and it allowed them to create and modify their plans quickly and efficiently.

These examples illustrate how easy it is to collect the information that is important to you. Virtually everyone in your organization is likely to be bombarded by useful information.

You just need to coach them to recognize and retrieve the information that is useful for your planning process. You don't need to hire additional staff or create an "Information Collection Department." The information is literally right in front of everyone in your company, every day. Unfortunately, many companies too often leave it right there instead of bringing it home.

Create successful strategies

Once the team has collected the information it needs, the next step is to create strategies that will achieve success. This can be a daunting task to some, but it is a source of pleasure for others.

To those managers that do not enjoy the process, we suggest that you identify and involve some capable team members who do. Alternatively, you may seek help from colleagues or from outside advisors. We believe that thinking strategically comes naturally to some people, and can be taught, with some difficulty, to others. If you can find those natural-born folks, grab them.

In an effort to simplify this process without diluting its importance, we've created a graphic representation for the creation of business strategies. This image on page 60 uses the successful activities of a spider as a metaphor for the creation of successful business strategies.

Be a spider

A spider creates a nearly invisible web to trap prey, and it senses the presence of the prey by the vibrations created by the struggling creatures that blunder into the trap. We like to mimic the spider by creating an information web, an affiliation of managers and staff that are constantly on the lookout for new developments. When new information is detected, the team assesses that information to determine if changes need to be made to existing strategies and plans.

Our web has four main sections, with various team members focused on each. Note that these four sections are represented by the four categories of information that we described earlier. This is information that you should be collecting and analyzing on a regular basis, not just once a year:

- The strengths and deficiencies of your company.
- Industry forces—the favorable and unfavorable trends in your industry.
- Your competitive environment.
- Your opportunities.

We've summarized this in a diagram that serves as a graphical check-list. It reminds you in a single glance of the information you must collect and assess and of the process of turning that information into strategies that will attain your goals. We call it the Spider Diagram because it has some resemblance to a spider and because it is constructed of a web—a web of information.

The Spider Diagram

Use the information wisely

Just like the spider that monitors her web, you should monitor your information web on a constant and regular basis, not just once a year. The interrelated information from the four key categories (the four outside ovals in the Spider Diagram) will present you with logical, and hopefully successful, options for the strategies you can create.

A Client's Story

One of our clients produced award-winning remodels for high-end residences. The firm was always searching for better marketing strategies.

One of the firm's designers noticed that the company's clients were highly impressed by the computerized drawings of their proposed work. They loved seeing the "finished product" before the project was even started.

The firm saw this as a big opportunity. Consequently, it acquired more advanced software that allowed clients to view their projects in 3-D and to "move around the room" at will, while viewing the project from any desired angle. The "wow factor" of this technology became a major selling tool for this firm in its proposal and design phases.

The Spider Diagram is a useful graphic for managers. It compels you to examine the current information in the marketplace and in your company, and it reminds you that this information may require that you change your strategies.

We suggest that you use this diagram frequently and regularly to assess your situation constantly. Doing this also has another significant benefit. Because you are collecting and analyzing information regularly to create adaptable strategies, you need not expend nearly as much time as you previously did on those once-a-year planning retreats.

We suggested earlier that you ask yourself and your team this question:

"What has changed in these four categories?"

Now you can ask a second question:

"In light of any changes in the four categories,
what should be our strategies?"

Chickens and eggs, strategies and goals

You'll notice that there is an arrow moving from the four information categories to strategies, and then from strategies to goals. Our view is that the information from the four categories determines the options available for creating viable strategies. Then, the strategies provide a picture of the "reasonable yet challenging" goals that you might attain.

This is in contrast to many people's view that goals are set first, then strategies are created to meet them. Which is correct? And why does it matter?

Actually, goals sometimes are set with seemingly no, or little, regard to the strategic options or to the current realities of the environment. And sometimes those goals are met.

Most famously, perhaps, is President Kennedy's promise, made in the early 1960s, to land a man on the moon by the end of the decade. When Kennedy made that promise, the country lacked many of the capabilities that would be needed to accomplish this, and he made a lot of government scientists quite nervous. But the promise was fulfilled with a few months to spare in the summer of 1969. Bravo!

More commonly, and more realistically for business owners, goals are set only after there is some understanding of the environment. If this were not the case, why even go through any type of planning process to collect and analyze information? It would instead be logical to simply set goals, then "just figure out a way to reach them."

We believe that even when companies profess to first set highly ambitious goals, and then devise strategies to reach them, that these goals are created with some basic knowledge of the strategies that will be effective in their marketplace. Some owners, however, might still say that's simply not so, we simply set the goals and then challenge our team to find out a way to accomplish them. Goals come first.

Let's look at a fictitious example to test this. Let's assume that we start a new business, a lunch-only sandwich shop in an average mall location, and that we have no knowledge of the restaurant business or the business environment (that's not as strange as it might sound).

We then contemplate what our revenue target and net profit goal should be for the coming year. Someone suggests that we could do $1 million in business and make 10 percent net profit. Then someone else, who has heard a talk by one of those "goals come first" folks, suggests that the business might just as well be ambitious and set a goal for $1 billion in business and 15 percent net profit. Maybe even $10 billion at 20 percent.

You can see that some knowledge is required to set meaningful goals. We surely wouldn't expect this sandwich shop to do anything close to those ambitious figures.

Even Kennedy had the benefit of some previous successful rocket launches to provide some basis for his admittedly ambitious challenge to the nation's scientists. Similarly, virtually all of us have some valuable information before we set goals. We might rely, for example, on last year's figures, the recent demise of an arch competitor, or some important change in the opportunities available to us to provide us with some basic guidance for setting the goals.

So, what do we actually do?

The reality is that most of us set goals and create strategies in an iterative process. We go back and forth to test the reasonableness of each.

For example, most of us always have some knowledge of our marketplace and our capabilities. In effect, we have some version of the Spider Diagram, however imperfect, in our mind.

Thus, based upon the available information, we create, in our minds, some rough but credible strategies that allow us to set a reasonable range for our goals. Then we set the specific goals, within this range. Finally, we create the detailed strategies we'll use to achieve the goals.

For example, in the case of our mall-based sandwich shop, we might know that there are five other lunch places in the mall, that we only have seating for 25 people at a time, that the average price per lunch is $7.50, and that we can turn over the tables approximately three times each lunch period. Based upon this information, we might set a revenue or profit goal for the shop, and then create the detailed strategies.

All the while, we might convince ourselves that we set goals and then created strategies. But it was only after we had enough knowledge of our available strategies that we were able to set the goals—in effect, to get ourselves in the ballpark of reasonable but challenging goals.

So why does this even matter? Why do we care whether strategies or goals come first?

The answer is that **the planning process makes logical sense only if we create strategies first.** Even if they are rough or imperfect strategies, we then use them to create a range within which goals are reasonable and challenging. Then, we set the specific goals. Finally, we create the detailed and more perfected strategies to attain those goals.

Thinking this way about the planning process is especially useful to your team. When they are observing your marketplace, assessing your internal capabilities, or exploring new opportunities, you want them to be using that information to formulate possible strategies for success. You want them to be thinking about what the organization will actually do in light of the changes that have occurred. You want them to be thinking strategically—all the time.

The current "great recession" is a case in point. Before the recession, many businesses were growing in size and profitability each year, with blue skies overhead. When the recession took hold, goals that might previously have been attained were no longer reasonable. This is because the previously available strategies were no longer available (for example, charge premium prices, sell only high-end goods) and because new strategies were often focused on survival (for example, create incentives just to get people to come into the store).

In effect, neither the old or the new strategies allowed most businesses to keep their previous goals in range. As a consequence, these businesses had to "change their expectations" under the current economic conditions.

The ability to set goals, then, is limited by the strategies that you can create. These in turn are determined by the capabilities of your organization and the external environment—those four major information categories described previously.

If this wasn't the case, you'd simply set the goals at astronomical levels, believing that somehow there existed a strategy to reach them. Pretty soon, you could become the gross domestic product of the entire country, all by yourself.

Modify the strategies in light of new information

If we make a visit late in the fiscal year to one of those one-in-20 firms that creates a business plan, we'll often encounter a flurry of activity. Goals will be established ("revenues will be 10 percent more than last year"), budgets will be assembled, and strategies will be created.

When it's all done, it often will carry an atmosphere of finality usually reserved for the conclusion of a successful root canal ("well, at least that's over"). This, of course, is exactly what we should expect.

After all, business owners have been taught for years that they should make a plan for the coming year, and the best time to do that is at the end of the previous year. And when it's done, they won't have to deal with it until next year. This notion is propagated by the use of a linear outline, such as the one we showed you a few pages back. It implies that there is a beginning and an end to the process, and that we can relax a bit after it's all done.

We know that the planning process, however, is a never-ending one. It goes around and around like a clock. And that's the way we like to think about it: a constantly moving process.

We've depicted this in the following diagram, titled The Business Planning Map. This diagram illustrates that the planning process goes around and around constantly. It only stops when you break away from the business (for example, when you sell or retire), and it requires your constant attention.

The Business Planning Map

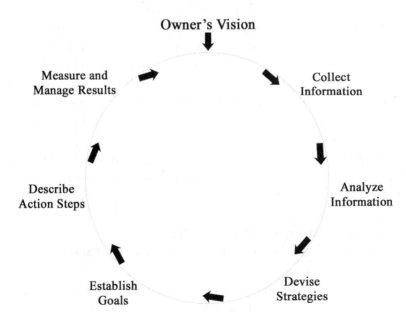

Like the sailboat captain who is constantly assessing his situation and creating new strategies, you can use your new information to constantly create new strategies for your business. You have an entire company of CIAs (Company Intelligence Agents) ferreting out relevant data. Now it's up to you to use that data to formulate a course of action.

Your planning activities must not wait for a once-at-the-end-of-the-year push. You must be doing this constantly, getting your CIAs constantly collecting information so that you can make corrections as needed. After all, your business runs by events, not a fiscal calendar.

By using the Spider Diagram as an updating tool, you can constantly detect changes in the environment that will affect your firm. As the information from your web is analyzed, you have the opportunity to create new strategies—strategies that will make you successful in your new environment. Like the spider, you should do this all the time; your environment doesn't change only at the time of your annual planning cycle. When you operate like this, you truly have the tools to be nimble and adaptable.

The real advantage of the Spider Diagram is to stimulate you to think about the planning process on a regular basis. The diagram is so simple that you'll memorize it easily, and you'll start to think about the effects of changes in your environment on any possible changes to your strategies.

Here's an analogy for this type of heightened awareness—in this case the awareness that planning is a constant process. If you close your eyes for a minute and try to recall all the blue items around you, you'll likely create a modest list. If you then open your eyes and look for blue items, the list likely will be much longer. After all, now you know what to look for: blue things. When you are aware of the constant importance of your planning process, and for the information that will build that process, you'll look for things that you never saw beforehand.

So now, with a heightened sense of awareness, you and your team can look constantly for new information needed to create new strategies and goals. You can simply use it to challenge your team to answer these three key questions:

1. What has changed in the four categories?
2. In light of any changes in the four categories, what should be our strategies?
3. In light of our available strategies, what is the range of values for our goals, which should be challenging yet reasonable?

—————————————— A Client's Story ——————————————

One of our clients, the owner of an engineering company, took all of his top managers to an off-site location for some team-building exercises. One of the exercises was to build a bridge over a ravine, using materials scattered in the woods.

Each person was given a card with a rule pertaining to the construction. These rules imposed very specific constraints on how the materials were to be handled and used. To complicate things further, additional rules were imposed as the team progressed in its activities.

It became obvious to a few participants that the materials to construct the bridge were not of uniform dimensions, thus requiring that they be positioned precisely, and in the right order, to complete the bridge. Because one of the rules precluded the handling of any material more than once, the location of each piece had to be carefully identified and planned well ahead of the placement of the first board.

The group performed flawlessly; they built a perfect bridge. But the important lesson they took home, articulated solely by them, was that they needed to marry their passion for perfection (they were engineers, after all) with an effective planning process. In fact, their planning took longer than the bridge building.

—————————————— A Client's Story ——————————————

One of our clients was a multi-store furniture retailer. The firm embraced the notion of ongoing planning, and they trained everyone to participate in the information collection process. They even had their delivery drivers involved, because the drivers were the customers' last touch with the company. The firm coached the drivers on collecting on-site customer feedback, and it also coached them to ask questions of the customers to clarify issues related to the delivery, set-up, use, and care of the furniture.

As a result of this process, one of the drivers realized that customers wanted an additional service: a warranty and protection program for their furniture. Although customers could obtain this service at the time of purchase, many of them apparently passed on the program when offered by the salesperson. Either because of reconsideration or further discussion with the delivery drivers, the customer became convinced that this was a useful service.

The firm realized that they could provide this service to customers at the time of delivery, and they immediately implemented a program to do so. They trained all the drivers on the new service, and they provided the necessary specialized equipment for all the delivery trucks. The potential benefits to the firm were so important that they also provided an incentive to the drivers for successful implementation.

After implementing this new program, the firm increased its customer loyalty as well as its profitability. Additionally, the morale and enthusiasm of the drivers increased noticeably, because they saw a real result from their participation in the process. In effect, they actually created a new process. Needless to say, the owners had smiles on their faces as well.

Both of these stories might prompt you to think about ways that you can harness the creativity of your entire team to generate similar ideas. Simply tell them your intentions, allow them to provide ideas, and thank and reward them for the ideas that you use.

Do this frequently

One of the major ways to make planning an effective process is to do it frequently. The key benefits of this are to make planning a habit rather than a dreaded once-a-year event, to create the ability to adapt quickly to changes in the environment, and to greatly reduce the time and effort required in any major once-a-year planning activity.

The Spider Diagram is a useful tool in making the process of planning a habit in your organization. It presents the four major types of information required, reminds you of the use of this information in creating strategies and goals, and does it all in one glance. It's an effective pictorial checklist.

At a minimum, we advise that you do this assessment monthly. After you do that for a while, the process will become comfortable enough that you'll be too anxious to wait another month and you'll want to do it weekly. After that, you'll find yourself thinking about it all the time. We suggest you drive the discussion through the Goal Management Team Meeting, which we discuss in the last chapter.

SURVIVAL OF THE FITTEST IDEAS

We concluded long ago that all successful businesses are not purposefully planned. Some are, for sure. Others seem to have somehow stumbled upon success, like winning the lottery.

When we looked closer at some of these "lottery wonders," we noticed something unexpected. Oftentimes it was a stroke of good fortune, or, as some of the owners might say, a single source of spontaneous brilliance, that eventually led to the company's overall success. Without that single event, the company likely would not have enjoyed the success it did.

These events often began as an inspiration or a small idea with no defined outcome. Sometimes they worked and sometimes they didn't.

We are big proponents of encouraging the development of these spontaneous ideas. There are just too many examples, in almost any business, of unforeseen fortune arising from seemingly meager ideas.

The evolution of these ideas into successful business activities mimics Darwin's theory of evolution. In this case, however, these ideas are vetted by the marketplace, and the "fittest" are the ones that survive.

This notion is a very useful tool to managers. It frees them from the perceived requirement that they somehow must anticipate successfully their every business decision. In fact, many managers are intimidated by the idea that they might somehow be punished for making a mistake.

Instead, it is actually useful if you consider your ideas to be "market mutations." These ideas are untried, outside your normal way of doing business, and perhaps even without any market research to justify them. They are, in essence, simply ideas that you think might work. They're experiments.

Now, here is where some discipline comes into the picture. You know from experience that you don't want to bet your entire company on some hair-brained new idea (despite the fact that there may be some rare and legendary companies that did just that).

But you might be willing to incubate these new ideas, as long as you establish some guidelines for success. So here are our guidelines:

1. Managing the Activity. You must have at least a minimum knowledge of how to manage the activity with your existing expertise, or else you have included in your budget and schedule the intent to acquire this expertise. You will not allow your core business to suffer while you attempt to learn how to manage an activity that is beyond your capabilities.

2. Financially Digestible Costs. The activity should be an acknowledged "company experiment." In the event that the experiment fails (and it will, in many cases), you have the financial robustness to absorb the costs. In such a case, you attempt to learn whatever you can from the experience.

3. Budget and Schedule. The overall company, or specific departments within the firm, should be given budget authority to conduct their experiments within a specified schedule or deadline. (You can't run the experiment forever.) Thus, the firm creates a budget designed to absorb these costs. In effect, these activities are internal research and development efforts, and you expect only a percentage of them to become successful.

4. Risk/Reward. A convincing case must be made that the potential rewards associated with this activity are justified by the risks. The person proposing the ideas knows that he or she doesn't know much (that's why it's an experiment in the spirit of a Darwinian mutation), but somehow is able to convince others that the company should proceed and try this. "It's worth a shot."

Your successful experiments may eventually play a significant role in your company. That's certainly one of your hopes. In fact, as your experiments come to fruition, or not, you will constantly examine and adapt your strategies and your goals.

—————————————— A Client's Story ——————————————

One of our clients was (and still is) a leader in residential mobile storage. They delivered a weatherproof container to the owner's home, provided the home owner as much time as needed to fill the container with items to be stored, and then returned to pick up the container and store it in their climate-controlled and secure warehouse.

Customers loved this service, and the company expanded rapidly nationwide. Then, a curious piece of information surfaced that would change the company's overall strategy.

Because of the company's presence in cities across the country, people storing their goods expressed a desire to their local manager to have the company move their possessions to another city to which they were moving. This idea was new to the company, and it was not the initial strategy of the firm.

The company examined the idea and decided that it met the previously mentioned four criteria. They had the expertise to manage the activity (several executives had moving experience), they could absorb a loss associated with trying this idea between two major cities, they created a budget and schedule for the activity, and they quantified the potential reward (large) and risk (small).

After some initial success, the firm revised its overall strategy and created logistics and financial plans to carry out this strategy. This included creation of a separate division to handle city-to-city moves nationwide and the establishment of monthly goals. That division quickly became the fastest growing and most profitable business unit in the firm, and it also promoted an ongoing relationship that enhanced customer loyalty.

The take-home message here is to think strategically all the time. Nurturing Darwinian experiments is just one means of creating and collecting information that can change your strategies. You also can use all of your employees, vendors, and customers to provide you with a never-ending stream of information that is constantly changing. Your challenge is to analyze that constantly changing information to determine where to go next.

Points to Remember

- The process of planning is more important than merely making a plan.

- Planning should be a regular ongoing process; not a once-a-year exercise.

- The process of planning is conceptually simple:
    1. Identify the information required for your plan.
    2. Engage everyone in information collection.
    3. Create successful strategies.
    4. Constantly create new strategies in light of new information.
    5. Do this frequently.

- Constantly monitor business conditions to detect changes in:
    - Market and industry trends.
    - Company strengths and weaknesses.
    - The competitive environment.
    - Opportunities.

- Constantly coach the team on how to collect and analyze useful information and to formulate strategies and goals.
- Don't be afraid to experiment with new ideas and strategies.
    - Actively manage the activity and the costs.
    - Understand the risks and rewards.
- Start doing it now!

CHAPTER 3

Coach the right people

A Fable

B ill Johnson was used to winning. And here he was again, in the thick of the competition, confident that once again he'd walk home with the championship. At his feet was the single object that stood between him and his fourth consecutive winning trophy.

It was a noodle—a huge noodle, at least a foot wide and 10 feet long, with fine drops of starch-laden moisture clinging to its edges. It was soft and supple, like a fine chamois cloth, a result of a full hour of boiling in the Competition Boiling Pot. Glistening in the sunlight, it lay on the ground at the foot of Competition Hill, just in front of Bill Johnson's feet.

As the King County Noodle Pushing Champion, he knew his way around noodles. After all, how many ways can there be around a noodle?

Bill circled the noodle, examining it from all sides. It was beautiful, and its starchy aroma hit him like the fragrance of an exotic flower.

Bill had seen plenty of noodles in his day. Big ones, small ones, domestic and foreign, thin ones and thick ones.

There was no doubt, however, that most people, including Bill, usually preferred the uncooked ones for competition. They had a strength and integrity to them that allowed the competitors to push and coax them in the right direction.

The wet ones, though, were an entirely different story. In fact, Bill had never successfully pushed a wet noodle up a hill. And he was King County Noodle Pushing Champion!

But there continued to burn in Bill Johnson a strong desire to prove that he could do this. He had always chosen uncooked noodles in his competitions, and he had become the county champion for three years in a row. In fact, he knew exactly the type of noodle that would ensure his success. He could spot a winning noodle a mile away.

Now, in the low light of the late afternoon, Bill stood over his wet noodle, evaluating his situation. The other competitors were already done for the day. They all had chosen uncooked noodles to push, and most of them had made it to the top of the hill, in widely varying times—times that Bill knew he could beat with a good uncooked noodle.

By choosing the wet noodle, however, Bill was going to show people that he was truly the best. He would out-push, out-coax, and out-noodle everyone. And he'd get extra points for succeeding with the wet noodle.

Bill was ready now. He got down on his knees and nuzzled up next to the knarly noodle.

As the crowd gasped, he assumed his legendary "knee-next-to-the-noodle" stance, a strategy that had served him well in all his other competitions. Taking a deep breath, imagining his success, Bill pushed for all he was worth.

Before he knew it, Bill was face down on the noodle, as helpless as a flopping mackerel. The noodle had simply bent when he pushed, and it assumed its same flat-to-the-ground appearance.

Bill tried again. And again. And again. All with the same result. He needed a new stance.

He tried pushing with his head, his feet, and even his stomach. He even tried the classic pasta pushing position taught to him by his father. All to no avail.

Then he tried something drastic. He took a deep breath and dove at the noodle, flapping his arms in a scooping motion in front of him. He looked like an oversized duck trying to go backward.

Bill thought that this new technique might be getting him somewhere, though, because his scooping and flapping motions actually pushed the noodle about 15 feet up the slope. But then he got so tired from the constant exertion that his arms cramped and he had to stop. Gravity pulled the wet noodle back down the hill, and it slithered back virtually to the starting point. Bill had gotten nowhere.

As Bill lay on the ground, trying to determine what to do next, the irony of the situation hit him full force. Here he was, totally exhausted from trying to move the wet noodle, while the noodle exerted no energy to move up the hill or even to resist Bill's efforts. It was just being a noodle.

In fact, the noodle actually took away Bill's energy. When Bill exerted himself to make some modest progress, the noodle squandered that energy by actually sliding down the hill! It was a one-way energy flow, with all the energy being sapped from Bill.

As time ran out for Bill, he felt at first a sense of despondence. He was disappointed that he wasn't going to earn another championship this year.

Then, he began to have a new sense of clarity and optimism. He realized that he was now crystal clear about his future. He knew that this would never happen again. His goal was to win at least two more championships, and he vowed to never again attempt to push a wet noodle up a hill.

He knew, of course, that he needed noodles of some kind to achieve those goals. He couldn't be the King County Noodle Pushing Champion without noodles.

The answer, then, was simple. Bill needed to pick the right noodles.

If he picked the right noodles and avoided the wrong noodles, he'd have lots of energy left over for hoisting his championship trophies. All of this was in his control, of course, if he just used his noodle.

NEVER TRY TO TEACH A PIG TO SING

In the previous story is Bill, one of our favorite guys. Bill learned that picking the right people, just like picking the right noodle, was the key to his success.

In Bill's earlier experiences, he did what many of us have done. He tried to work with the wrong people. He may have done this for any number of reasons: No one else was around, the person had been with the company for a long period of time, or perhaps the person would finally "see the light" and do a really fine job. Bill's belief was that he could save these people and make them into high performers. Bill was certain that he could turn a person who was a lost cause into a blazing success (like he tried to do with the wet noodle).

One of our strong beliefs is that each of us can succeed if we're in the right position, and each of us can fail if we're in the wrong position. This is a bit heretical, because oftentimes we tend to view people as successful or not, high achievers or not, big contributors or not. Consequently, we also conclude that these "good" people can do anything for us and that the "bad" people can hardly do anything well.

There certainly are some folks who have a broad range of capabilities and can do many things well. You'd probably view these folks as stars in your organization. Conversely there are folks with a more limited range of capabilities, people who have limited activities in which they can perform well. You might view these folks as somehow less valuable to your organization, even if they truly excelled at certain activities for which they were best suited.

A Client's Story

One of our clients employed a group of top electrical and mechanical engineers who designed industrial machinery. We interviewed these top engineers to gain some insight on the qualities they possessed that made them so good at what they did. This is what one of them told us.

"I love the details," he told us. "I love to match each product to each specification number to ensure that every single item is correct. I know that this would be boring to some people, but it's not at all boring to me. I love everything to be right, and it's interesting to me to get everything right. I don't get tired doing this."

A Client's Story

Another of our clients was a partner in a professional services firm, in a highly technical discipline. To complete the day-to-day work and meet the expectations of the client required great attention to detail, and errors were costly for the firm as well as the client.

This partner's primary job was to develop business with new clients. He was one of those gifted individuals who can start a conversation with anyone, and who not only feels comfortable doing this but actually thrives on it. In effect, he's never met a stranger.

If you ask him what makes him so good at what he does, this is what he tells you:

"I love meeting people and determining what they are trying to accomplish, determining their goals. Then I bring the resources together to create a plan for meeting those goals. Then I leave the execution to the technical people, and I go on to do it again with a new client. I never worry about the details, only the big picture, and that's what I love."

So here we have the stories of two exceptional individuals who excelled at what they did. But neither could do an even acceptable job at the other person's position. In effect, we'd call them failures if they switched roles, and we'd probably invite them to leave our company.

In fact, when we take people ill-suited to a position and force or cajole them to attempt to excel at that position, we only frustrate ourselves and annoy them. There is a contemporary metaphor for this: *Never try to teach a pig to sing. The music is terrible and it annoys the pig*.

But when we look at companies across the country, all too often we see people in roles for which they are ill-suited. In some cases they are ignored as low achievers; in other cases their managers continue to "train" them, attempt to motivate them, and continue to give them below-average performance reviews. It's hard to find a winner here, isn't it?

We think that part of this frustrating scenario is due to our culture. The American culture is complex and powerful, but among its attributes are an enduring optimism and a belief that we can accomplish almost anything. Even a brief look at our history shows a country that defied the odds in its creation, triumphed over overwhelming adversities over the centuries, and created an enduring form of government and a prosperous business climate that has attracted people from around the world for decades. Who wouldn't want to be a part of that?

This message continues to be reinforced even today. We have television and movie stars, celebrities, and athletes telling us that we too can achieve success, as they have, if we only believe in ourselves and stick to it. The equation is something like desire plus perseverance equals success. If only it were true.

The belief that it is true explains, at least in part, why managers ignore natural abilities when putting individuals in the wrong role. They simply don't consider the notion that there is a wrong role. The individual would be successful if she only applied herself, worked harder, showed some ambition and initiative, and so forth. They even use elaborate checklists in the employee's performance review, ranked on a scale of one to 10, to document the various characteristics that are holding this person back from attaining success.

Now don't get us wrong here. We think the enduring optimism of our country and our belief that we can accomplish great things, are positive and powerful attributes of our culture and our individual character.

We don't believe, however, that we can all succeed in any role, as long as we have enough desire and perseverance. And we don't believe that our failure in the wrong role is due simply to a lack of desire or character.

Unfortunately, there are too many instances of people in positions for which they simply aren't suited. Sometimes they put themselves in these situations, and in other instances a manager puts the person in the wrong role, a role in which success is virtually unattainable.

A Client's Story

One of our clients was an expert company in a highly technical field. The employees had years of specialized training, and their successful engagement with clients, with whom they usually worked one-on-one, was dependent upon their expertise.

One of the best of the staff members decided that he wanted a managerial position in the company, a position that would require him to oversee other staff. This was a dubious decision because this employee lacked the obvious social and coaching abilities required.

Nevertheless, he was offered the position. After all, he'd been a high-performing staff member. Didn't he deserve this promotion?

Despite numerous coaching talks from his boss, course corrections from the company's owner, and feedback from his subordinates and even clients, the employee never could attain an acceptable level of performance as a manager. No surprise there.

Unfortunately, in the previous scenario, the company tried to teach a pig to sing. Make no mistake, the employee was a high performer, a highly respected technical contributor to the firm, and an all-around good guy with no pig-like qualities. He just had no business in a managerial role. He finally admitted this to himself and to his CEO, returned to his role as a member of the technical staff, and once again had a happy time in his day-to-day activities.

There are many instances such as this—instances where someone takes on a role for which he or she is ill suited. Sometimes it is done out of necessity, such as when someone feels that they simply need a paying job. Sometimes it occurs when managers put folks in the wrong spot.

In the case of a management position, culture again plays an important role. We've all been taught from an early age that being the leader, the one in charge, or the boss is a rightly ambitious road to success. So folks aspire to management, even when they don't fit the position.

A person in the wrong role is usually a prescription for failure. You might wonder why we used the word *usually*, when it seems logical that if the person is in the wrong roles, things simply won't work.

In fact, sometimes people function in the wrong role for reasonably long periods of time, and they may even achieve high levels of success. Unfortunately, a person in that role—the wrong role—simply must expend a great deal of energy and attention to operate in a way that is contrary to his or her natural inclinations or abilities. Maintaining this level of energy and attention usually cannot be sustained indefinitely without inducing some form or stress, resignation, or failure.

A True Story

We once had a client whose "significant other" was a star salesperson at a well-known upscale national retail chain. He described her as a naturally introverted person, but he told us with real pride about her success as a salesperson, a role that required her to create new and ongoing relationships with perfect strangers who came into the store.

The more he described her, the more we wondered if she was in the wrong role. In similar situations, we'd observed that folks like this, when placed in a "highly social" position, came home stressed. They just wanted to be left alone to "decompress" and "relax."

He confirmed that this was the case. She didn't want to talk to him for about an hour after getting home; she wanted to spend time alone, in the quiet.

Note that if she were naturally inclined to be a relationship builder and highly social, she'd probably talk his ear off over dinner telling him about what a great day she had. She'd be in a position that she loved. That was not the case.

Shortly after we had this conversation, she left the company to seek a new position.

There is yet another perspective on this. Consider someone in a position in which they are viewed as a mediocre performer: They're doing okay, but certainly not excelling.

This might be due to any number of reasons including lack of effort, training, or management direction. It might also be due to being in the wrong position. The person's modest achievements, therefore, might simply be a reflection of her attempts to perform in the wrong role.

——————————— A True Story ———————————

Michael Jordan was one of the greatest basketball players of all time. In his role as a player, he outshined virtually all other players, each of whom was an exceptional athlete.

Shortly after an announced retirement, Jordan decided to become a professional baseball player. This seemed like a realistic possibility; he was truly an outstanding athlete with extraordinary agility, hand-eye coordination, and quickness. He could jump pretty well, too.

He was given a spot on one of the minor-league teams, with the expectation that he'd work his way to the big leagues. It never happened. Despite his elite level abilities in basketball, Michael Jordan never progressed beyond the minor leagues in baseball. For him, baseball was the wrong role.

And so it is for all of us. There are places where we each can be successful, and places where we each can be mediocre or even fail. Our quest should be to find the role or position that takes advantage of our natural abilities, so that we can do the things we do best. In such cases, it will be relatively easier and more enjoyable for us, performing at a higher level will come naturally, and it won't require lots of "management."

MATCHING PEOPLE TO THE POSITION

So, how can you find a winner for the position you want to fill? Two of the major responsibilities of a great manager are to find the right people to fill the positions needed and to coach those people to a high level of achievement. This is the essence of coaching the right people: to first identify the right people, and then to coach them to achieve their goals.

There are three steps required:

1. Define the position and the skills and abilities needed.
2. Find the person with the right skills and abilities.
3. Coach them to excellence.

Define the position

It seems almost too easy to state that the first step in this process is to define the position. That's what everyone already does, isn't it? They determine that they need a salesperson, write some type of job description, and then go looking.

Unfortunately, a key part of the process that we've often found missing is the link between the company's vision, goals, and strategies and the position being filled. All too often, companies simply replace a person who has left, or another salesperson is added to the existing structure, or a new management position is created when the group gets to a certain size. In other words, they lose sight of the big picture, the picture that tells them what they need to do today to get to where they want to be tomorrow.

This is actually quite understandable and, in many cases, seems to reflect common sense. It even echoes the cliché "If it ain't broke, why fix it?" Why continually invent new positions when we already know what needs to be done? Why not add another salesperson when we've just seen our sales grow rapidly over the last two years? Why not add another manager when the group gets to twice the size of the other groups?

There are many examples illustrating how positions have been filled at the expense of the company's future success—of losing sight of the big picture. There seem to be two major reasons for this.

In the first case, companies seem to be making a last-ditch effort in a losing cause. They continue to do what they've been doing, even though the future is sending them warning signals.

For example, there are many local video rental companies that have continued to plan for the future as if it's still 1995. They have acted oblivious to their declining sales due to the obvious encroaching forces of firms that deliver movies and entertainment by Internet and retail kiosks.

Similarly, logging firms have lobbied hard to have the right to cut the last 1 percent of old-growth timber in the country. What will they do after that? And Kodak continued to try to build its film business for years after the advent of digital imaging.

Our main point here is that it's very easy to continue to do what you've always done. It worked in the past, and it requires little thought and expense. So, maybe you can ride the pony for just a little bit longer and then figure something out after that. Good luck.

In the second case, companies appear to be oblivious to their changing environment. Instead of ignoring some clear and obvious signals, they simply don't see any signals.In such cases, we believe that they fail to implement an effective planning process. They fail to collect and analyze information about their environment that would allow them to create successful strategies to fulfill their vision.

For example, a research division of the Xerox Company was responsible for inventing and developing some of the key innovations now commonly used on virtually all computers, but the company made virtually no effort to commercialize them. Xerox didn't see the potential importance of these innovations, perhaps because it was focused on imaging rather than on computer technology.

Whatever the reason, these innovations apparently were not identified as opportunities (a key component of an effective planning process). Many years later, Xerox awoke to the commercial opportunities it had missed, and it sued Apple, who was implementing some of these technologies. But the statute of limitations had expired and the suit was unsuccessful. Too late.

Similarly, recyclers of newspapers might not immediately understand that their shrinking business is due to declining readership of papers, and attorneys might not understand that their business decline is due to the effectiveness of huge and effective advertising campaigns by a few large firms. All these companies are typically focused on the job at hand (the day-to-day activities of the business) rather than possible signals from the marketplace. As a consequence, they might continue to hire and plan as they had done in the past, only to be rudely awakened.

These examples illustrate that the position you seek to fill should be linked to your vision, strategies, and goals rather than to your day-to-day activities of the past. After you've engaged in an effective planning process, you will be able to identify the positions needed to carry out your strategies and attain your goals and vision.

Now you can look more closely at describing the position you seek to fill. We advise that you actually write out the requirements for the position, giving it the care and planning it deserves. After all, you're going to be bringing someone new into the position, which has significant implications for that individual as well as others in your organization, for however long they remain.

There are several key components to an effective position description. At a minimum it should be clear and unambiguous, and it also should set clear expectations for the employee and the manager about the definition of success for the position (the goals).

On the following pages is an example of a position description. We'll explain some of this later when we talk about a management system for your company. For now, we'll summarize the parts that most directly affect your ability to actually define the position.

One thing we'd like to stress here is that a position description is not the same as a traditional job description, which describes tasks. Position Descriptions focus on *goals*.

POSITION DESCRIPTION
Chief Estimator

Title: Chief Estimator

Department: Building Demolition

Direct Supervisor: VP Operations

Position Purpose: Manage all demolition estimating and sales efforts to maximize our corporate sales and profitability and enhance our image.

Goals:

- Achieve gross margin on projects won of at least 28%.
- Bid on work that comprises at least 60% of our market.
- Maintain our success/bid ratio at 25% or higher.

Responsibilities:

- Recruit, hire, train, retain, motivate, and manage a competent estimating team, and maintain effective departmental and interdepartmental communication and accountability.
- Maintain a sufficient bid volume and win ratio to support company sales objective.
- Attain an average score of 4 or higher on client surveys.
- And so forth….

Major Challenges:

- Winning bids in a very highly competitive industry.
- Working with a variety of rough-and-tumble subcontractors.
- Estimating costs on projects that have no precedent—unique situations.

- Treating everyone as an individual to extract great performance.
- Satisfying clients that are often very demanding and discerning.

Authority:
Act Alone:

- Incur expenses according to established budget.
- Set margins and close bids for projects up to $100,000.

Touch Base with Supervisor or President:

- Discretionary rewards up to $1,000 per quarter.
- Set margins and close bids for projects up to $300,000.

Need Approval from Supervisor or President:

- Expenses beyond budget.
- Rewards in excess of $1,000 per quarter.
- Set margins and close bids for projects over $300,000.

Performance Evaluation Criteria

- Comparison of actual performance to the goals for this position.
- Fulfillment of the responsibilities for this position.

Performance Evaluation Schedule
- Annual review.
- Quarterly goal review.
- Weekly one-on-ones.

Qualifications:

- Ten (10) years of experience in Estimating/Construction Management, demolition industry estimating experience is preferred but not necessarily required.
- College degree in Construction Management, Engineering, or related field is advantageous but not required.
- Intermediate to advanced computer skills including Word, Excel, Access.
- Proven ability to prioritize, organize, and delegate responsibility.
- Proven leadership, management, interpersonal, and team-building skills.
- Excellent oral and written communication skills.
- Excellent negotiating skills.
- Excellent business references.

Compensation: Exempt, salaried, paid weekly, business expenses, and automobile allowance.

Work Schedule: 50 to 60 hours per week, depending on workload, is

anticipated.

This is, however, a challenging and demanding position, and it is crucial to our success. We expect that the person in this position will devote whatever time is required to ensure their success, as well as that of the company.

There are five parts of the position description of highest importance in actually defining the position. These include:

1. **Purpose.**
2. **Goals.**
3. **Responsibilities.**
4. **Major challenges.**
5. **Qualifications.**

The **purpose** of the position refers to the reason that the position even exists. Why, for example, do we have an estimator position? By stating the purpose of the position you'll clarify the mission of that position—why it exists—and provide the employee with a strong focus.

The **goals** of the position refer to the individual goals we described in the first chapter. In our example here, the position has three goals, all of which are measurable and clear.

The **responsibilities** are all those day-to-day activities that must be accomplished in the position. This provides clarity as well as sets proper expectations for the person in the position. These are usually not quantified or measured on an individual basis, like the goals, but rather are considered as a whole when the manager coaches the person in the position. You'll notice that at the fourth bullet in the description we wrote "And so forth," because the list of responsibilities could be quite long and will be specific to your organization.

The **major challenges** section describes why this position can't be accomplished by your dog. It states the major internal and external factors that threaten success in the position, thus creating appropriate expectations for the employee and the manager.

Finally, the **qualifications** section explains the experience, skills, and knowledge that we expect from the person in this position. We urge you to think carefully about the true requirements for the position, because it is common to merely recite a list of common attributes. For example, managers frequently specify that a college degree is needed, when a person without such a degree could excel at the position.

You might choose to use two slightly different versions of the position description. One version would be for the candidates, providing them with clear direction on the position and its goals. It would contain all the information we described. The second version would be for internal purposes, and this version would include more detail on the qualifications you seek for the person who successfully will fill the position.

More specifically, the details on qualifications that you'll describe for your internal use, and that you'll leave off the candidate's position description, relate to the candidate's natural abilities. You'll want to discover for yourself whether they have all the natural abilities you seek.

The reason for this is that you can't simply list the required natural abilities and then ask candidates whether they possess them. They'll simply tell you they do. They want the job, they've figured out what you want, and they're smart enough to tell you what you want.

In fact, there likely are a number of natural abilities that would carry a person to success in any given position. In defining the position, therefore, you must be as conscientious at identifying these natural abilities as you are about defining the skills and experience needed.

In many cases, a person's natural abilities are more important than a resume in predicting their success. For example, you can teach them the on-the-job stuff, but you can't instill a new attitude.

This may have been said best by Herb Kelleher, the founder of Southwest Airlines. He confidently preached: "Hire for Attitude." He believed that the employees of Southwest Airlines could be taught what they needed to know about their role in the airline business, but that they already had to possess a positive attitude. And Southwest Airlines couldn't teach employees how to get that attitude.

As another example, a love for details was critical for that engineering position we described above. This isn't something that the company could teach him; that engineer we described somehow came all packaged up with this love of details. So, when the company goes looking for another great engineer for a similar position, it likely will increase its chances of finding the right person if they find someone who also has this love for details.

Alternatively, the company managers wouldn't want to hire someone for that engineering position who must be pushed every day to check the details. They'll just keep finding mistakes, trying to coach the new person to do something she doesn't enjoy, providing her with plenty of negative signals, and writing her poor performance reviews.

Instead, the managers want someone who is going to excel at the task and who thinks doing detail work is fun. They want someone who has this natural ability—this love for details. If they find this person, they'll hardly have to supervise her. She'll look forward to doing her job, and she'll take pride in doing it well.

Find the right person

Finding the right person is the most difficult of the three activities here. Virtually every business has hired a "terrific new employee" only to later discharge "a terrible employee." Some business owners have even resigned themselves to the notion that the entire interview process is little more than a crap shoot—you do your best and then fire the ones that don't work out.

There are, of course, numerous methods and processes for identifying and interviewing candidates. In fact, there are many companies that have been founded for the sole purpose of assisting business owners in the hiring of good employees. They practice their craft through books, on-line surveys and questionnaires, and in-person interviews and coaching.

We encourage you to talk with colleagues to identify any of these firms that have proven themselves. And we encourage you to work with the best of these firms to assist you in finding great employees. You'll need all the help you can get, because this is anything but a science.

Our own experience has proven that there is at least one significant thing we can do to increase our ability to find the right person for a position. We need to determine if his or her natural abilities are well suited to the position we seek to fill.

Remember that list of natural abilities that we told you to include on your internal version of the position description? This is where it comes into play. For example, you might seek someone who loves working with numbers, or who loves meeting and engaging new people, or who loves creating new strategies when conditions change. Now the challenge is to find candidates that possess those natural abilities.

This is, unfortunately, not a straightforward task. If you ask candidates if they possess these abilities, they likely will put on their "great interviewee" hat and tell you that they do. Consequently, you need to find a non-obvious means of identifying these individuals.

———————————— A Client's Story ————————————

One of our clients sought great managers for its nationwide network of nearly 20 offices. Historically, the firm had great difficulty in finding the right people to manage these offices, and turnover and frustration were high.

We helped them define and detect the natural abilities needed for an excellent city manager. We did this by interviewing the great managers (and only the great managers) currently in residence at the firm, with the purpose of detecting the natural abilities that made them so successful in their position.

We first asked the managers to identify the natural abilities they possessed that made them so successful. Then, we asked them about the activities that pleased them in both their personal and work life to gain further clues about their natural abilities. When we completed the interviews, we had identified several natural abilities in common to all the great managers.

The next step in the process was the most difficult. We needed to create questions for the candidates that would detect the natural abilities we sought. But the questions had to be "non-obvious," because candidates might simply tell us what they thought we wanted to hear.

Oftentimes, the managers we interviewed gave us the best hints or ideas for formulating the questions. Other times, we simply had to be creative, formulate our questions, and then test them on the managers we interviewed to see how they might answer. Then we coached our client on how to use them with the candidates they interviewed.

For example, one of the natural abilities identified by the managers was a strong work ethic. We knew that we couldn't ask candidates if they had a strong work ethic; of course they'd say they did. We needed an indirect means of determining this.

Here is what we formulated: "Tell me about your earliest work experience." When candidates answer, they assume that we are merely curious or that we might want to know if their early work experience is related to their career.

What we have found, however, is that people who started working at a young age (say, age 16 or younger) learned a work ethic that stayed with them. We don't really care what they did, as long as it was real work and they did it early in life.

Although we don't think this question is foolproof, it has been remarkably reliable at indicating a strong work ethic. (Try it yourself by asking this question of people that you know who possess a strong work ethic, or who don't.) Our clients have used it to great advantage.

When we completed this assignment, we had formulated questions for each of the identified natural abilities. In some cases, we created two or more questions for a single ability. In all cases, we created a series of indirect questions that our client could pose to his candidates to detect the presence of the desired natural abilities for the position.

Once again, we won't tell you that this is foolproof. But our client did experience a significant improvement in the quality and retention of the newly hired managers, and the process has worked well for other clients. We believe that this process can work for virtually any position in any firm.

You can see that this process was not entirely logical. We tried to devise questions or situations to which there were not easily discernable answers. We tried to get the candidates to reveal their *natural abilities* without asking them directly.

This client experience is described more fully in Appendix C. In that section we've provided you with detailed guidance on the process of actually creating the questions that are focused on specific natural abilities.

It's important to realize that a natural ability that might serve us well in one environment might be a real liability in another environment. We shouldn't think of these abilities as inherently good or bad. Instead, we need to look at the suitability of these natural abilities for a particular position or environment.

As an example, let's go back and pick on that great engineer again. His love for details allows—indeed, compels—him to be successful in his current environment. We'd be hard pressed to find a better person for the position. But what if the position were different?

Let's imagine that because of his excellence at his current position, the engineer's boss decides to promote him to become the manager of engineering. The boss might do this for a variety of reasons: put the engineer in a position where he can directly influence other engineers, reward him for a job well done, justify a higher salary with a commensurate title, set a great example, and so forth.

Sometimes, this actually works. People are promoted to a managerial position because they've excelled at their current position, and they turn out to be great managers.

Many times, however, it simply does not work. And when that manager of engineering doesn't live up to expectations ("Just what is he thinking?"), his supervisors rely on negative feedback and discipline to remedy the situation: continually pointing out mistakes, providing plenty of negative signals, and writing a poor performance review.

So what happened? Why didn't this guy perform as expected?

The reason is that the natural abilities required to be a great manager are significantly different than the natural abilities to be a great engineer. In fact, we believe that these differences are as great as if the engineer changed careers—which is exactly what he did!

Being a great engineering manager is an entirely different career from being a great engineer. And the natural abilities that compel someone to succeed as a manager are different from the abilities that compel that person to succeed as an engineer.

This scenario is a common one—played out across businesses every day. So, is it wrong to promote people to management after they've done a good job in their position? It's not wrong at all, as long as you've determined that the person has the abilities needed to be a great manager.

For example, you might determine that the managerial position you seek to fill requires strong coaching skills (among other things). If your crack engineer is a great coach (he loves to coach and does it well), he might be a strong candidate for the manager's position (assuming he has the other abilities you seek). If he's disdainful of being a coach, and merely expects everyone to "listen to what I tell them and then do a good job, that's what we pay them to do," you likely will do well to keep him away from your management ranks.

The vital need is to hire those with the right abilities for each of the positions in your company. You shouldn't "just get a warm body in here" or "just get someone who can do the basics" if you intend to create a great company.

Remember: Those who possess the "wrong" abilities for a position may be perfectly suited for some other position. It may be another position in your company, or it may be in a company other than yours. Coaching these individuals in the "wrong" position may produce some small improvements, but these individuals will most likely never attain the high level of performance that comes naturally to those with the right abilities.

A Client's Story

One of our clients created high-end customized software for a wide variety of businesses. The company was filled with highly educated computer specialists, and they worked very hard to produce exceptional products and build the company's growing reputation.

The company also contained a team of "customer care" specialists. This team maintained the day-to-day relationships with existing clients, providing them with product support, training, and ongoing guidance that would help their businesses run successfully.

Meanwhile, in the back offices of the company, with a smile that would light up entire rooms, was a person who worked in the accounting department. This woman was highly responsible and attentive to detail, all of which made her very effective as a part of the accounting team.

There was only one problem: This woman desperately wanted to be part of the customer care team. She had held similar positions in previous companies, but she had signed on in this new accounting role to secure a much-needed job with a growing and exciting firm.

This woman's natural inclination to be in a people-focused activity was obvious to all who knew her. Her strong sense of responsibility, close attention to detail, and natural abilities in dealing with people made a killer combination for the customer care position.

She expressed her desires to the owners and top managers of the firm, and they listened politely. But they had no intention of allowing her to move out of her accounting position.

"She does her job too well," they said. "We can't let her leave her current position." Their highest levels of creativity were embodied in the ways that they denied this change to occur.

We're sure that you can see where this is headed. The woman became increasingly discouraged and frustrated, and she left the firm.

This company missed a great opportunity. They could have placed this talented individual in a role that would have played to her natural abilities—a role in which she would have thrived and excelled. She would have come to work every day energized and excited, and the company would have received these benefits without having to lift a finger. (How many times have you heard folks anguishing about how to improve morale or motivate employees?)

In the end, of course, the managers were required to replace her anyway. She made the decision for them. They lost an exceptional individual, and they spent much unneeded time filling her now-vacated position.

Most interestingly to us, stories like this are common, although not always quite as obvious. The challenge for great managers, and the one at which these managers failed, is to identify the natural abilities of their team members and to place them in positions where they can use those abilities on a regular basis.

The search for people with the right abilities is a key responsibility of the manager, whereas the actual execution of the work required for the position is the key focus of the employee. As shown in the following illustration, both the manager and the employee are involved every step of the way, but the manager's role moves from director to coach once the goals are established.

Manager and Employee Focus

Early on, the manager's primary focus is to define the position and then seek to fill the position from the available pool of candidates. Then the manager chooses the right person and clearly communicates the goals of the position to that new employee.

After this point, the employee's primary focus is to execute the work required for the position and to acquire new skills, if possible, to adjust to changing needs. Although the employee likely will not attain any new natural abilities, she can acquire new skills to improve her chances of attaining some new position within the firm.

It is during these later activities that the manager's role focuses on coaching. Now that the manager has chosen the right person and clearly communicated the goals for the position, the manager coaches the employee to attain those goals and to acquire new skills.

The previous diagram might imply that hiring a new person into the company is the preferred solution. This may not always be the case, especially when the company has someone in a position that is particularly difficult to fill.

A Client's Story

One of our clients designed and built restaurants, team stores, and meeting places for high-traffic venues such as sports stadiums, malls, and theme parks. They did superb work, and their designs compelled people to enter the venues.

The company's chief salesperson was outstanding. He turned a new prospect into an enthusiastic customer in record time. He had a gift—a natural ability—for creating strong relationships and gaining trust with virtually everyone he met. And he could think on his feet to tailor his presentations to every client's unique situation. He was a star.

The company's first thought was to hire another star like this, so that the company could grow even faster. If one of these guys was good, two would be great.

But then, a different solution came to mind. Instead of trying to find another star, which would be very difficult indeed, perhaps the answer was to find more time for the current sales guy—more time for him to focus on creating those relationships and closing sales.

And that's what the company did. They assigned an assistant to the sales guy, someone who already worked for the company and could easily attend to the administrative details, paperwork, and follow-up that the sales guy hated and didn't do well. This provided the sales guy with more pure selling time, which he loved. And now he could generate twice as much in sales. It was a winning solution.

Coach them to excellence

So, it's now obvious that the third requirement for coaching the right people is to be a great coach. But what does that mean? How can you be a great coach? And why would you want to be a coach. Isn't this about management?

Some True Stories

What do Vince Lombardi, Jack Welch, and Andrew Cioffi have in common?

Vince Lombardi was one of the greatest-ever professional football coaches. His reputation for extracting the best from his men is legendary, and his players were fiercely loyal to him. They admit that Lombardi was a tough taskmaster, but he compelled them to perform at levels beyond their own expectations.

Jack Welch won praise for years as arguably the best CEO of the 1990s. He grew GE to unprecedented heights, and he did it while grooming his own successor and his executive team to achieve high levels of success on their own.

Andrew Cioffi is a father of three boys, and he's one of the best coaches we know. (He just happens to be one of our brothers—amazing coincidence.) He doesn't supervise a football team or a Fortune 100 Company, but he does extract amazing performance from those three boys.

What makes these guys such great coaches?

What makes Andrew such an outstanding coach is his intuitive and insightful understanding of each of his boys. He first sees, in a surprisingly objective way, the strengths and natural talents of each of his sons, and he then treats each of them in a unique way so that they can best use the talents they possess.

This is what Lombardi and Welch did, of course, only on a more global athletic and corporate stage. They recognized the natural talents of each of their team members, intuitively nurtured those talents, and coached each person to achieve high goals by treating each one as the unique individual they were.

Why don't we all do this?

Perhaps the best answer is that most of us have a culturally ingrained response to fix things that appear to be broken. When we encounter people who have clear weaknesses, we want them to improve those weaknesses, and sometimes they spend a majority of their time trying to do so.

But great coaches (and great managers) know that *the greatest benefits come from allowing a person to exercise his or her natural strengths and abilities.* These coaches clearly define the goals to be achieved, but then they allow people to achieve the goals in their own way. That means that each person must be treated differently, not the same, and that the coach must nurture the talents that each person possesses.

So the challenge here is to understand people's talents and to put them in a role that allows them to use those talents frequently. They'll love the role they're in, they'll perform at a high level, and both the manager and the employees will have great fun and a sense of true accomplishment in attaining their goals.

The Manager and Employee Focus diagram we showed you on page 94 indicates that an important role for an effective manager is to pick the right people for the position and to coach them to achieve their goals. That is the essence of the manager-as-coach. It's a talent search followed by goal-setting, providing overall direction, and training so that the employee and the team reach their goals.

There are, of course, many styles and means of managing, ranging from a strict autocracy ("It's my way or the highway, Sparky. Just do what I tell you to do.") to a state of totally hands off ("You guys all seem like free spirits, and I don't like managing, so just figure out what needs to be done"). However, if you are to attain your vision and goals, we think that you'll want to take full advantage of the natural abilities of people who are best suited to the positions in your organization while also ensuring that they're moving in the right direction.

This diagram illustrates the match between employee and managerial styles that we believe best suits a coaching style of management. It takes full advantage of each person's natural abilities, their desire to attain goals, and the manager's desire to assist them in attaining those goals.

The Empowerment Sweet Spot

On the left side of the diagram, employee styles are on a continuum, ranging from a desire for a high degree of direction or control on the bottom, to a desire for virtually no management of any kind at the top. You've probably seen folks who span this entire range. The want-high-control individuals are the ones that say things like "Just tell me what you want each day and I'll do it for you." The want-no-control folks say things like "I know what to do, and I don't need any manager to tell me what to do."

Along the bottom of the diagram, managerial styles range from autocrat to hands off, and you've likely seen this range as well. The autocrat is a micromanager, involved in all aspects of everyone's day. The hands-off manager lets folks do whatever they want to do, with no goals or expectations of agreed-upon outcomes.

Somewhere near the mid-point of the employee and managerial ranges are two lines that intersect in the middle of a heart. We hope you'll indulge our imagery, but we believe that there can be true empowerment in your organization when you have a proper alignment of employee and managerial styles. This occurs when both employees and managers agree that the employees should have clear goals to attain as well as the freedom to attain those goals in their own way. Thus, the hearts and minds of the employees and the managers are aligned.

For those managers inclined to provide very little direction, believing that folks will simply do the right thing, we caution you. Our experiences with clients, as well as polls and surveys of companies around the country, indicate that many employees do not know their goals or the company's goals. To paraphrase Yogi Berra, it's hard to reach your goals if you don't know what they are.

And remember, too, that the company goals should represent progress in attaining the company's vision. If you're not attaining such goals, your vision will just be an unattainable dream.

For those managers with a tendency to micromanage, try this. Hold your hand up in front of you, as if you're trying to stop traffic. Then ask someone facing you to do the same. Then press your hand against his, and push slightly against him. Then push harder. We can predict with virtual certainty that he'll push back. No matter how hard you push, he'll meet you with equal or even greater resistance.

Remember here that you didn't ask him to resist you or to push against you; you merely asked him to hold his hand up like yours. We believe that it is natural for people to push back. They do it in this exercise (not once has a person failed to push back, in all the years we've done this), and they do it in the workplace, sometimes overtly and sometimes in more subtle ways. But people generally do not like being pushed.

So, as a manager, you have a choice. You can prove to them that you can push harder, or you can simple find a way to harness their natural abilities so that pushing is not required. In the latter case, they'll do what comes naturally, and they'll do it well and without much of your supervision. And you'll be able to do things other than push.

---------------------- A Friend's Story ----------------------

Years ago, we went fly fishing with one of our friends, Paul, and his two sons, Garrett and Kyle, who were about 10 and 8 years old, respectively. They both had been fishing with their dad on previous occasions, and they knew how to cast a line, maintain a low presence at the stream edge, and find the likely fishing holes.

Garrett was quite an accomplished fisherman, but the younger Kyle needed some assistance in tying some of the more difficult knots in his line. He asked his dad to help him.

What transpired next was a coaching miracle. Paul stood beside his son, and clearly and calmly talked him through the steps to tie the proper knots. He never once touched Kyle's pole or line, nor did he chastise Kyle in any way. Instead, he methodically guided Kyle through the steps needed to tie each knot, giving him encouragement at every opportunity, and letting Kyle do it in his own way.

Additionally, Paul did all this in a way that was both fun and instructive for everyone watching. Both the coach and the student had a great time throughout this interchange. It was clear that Paul enjoyed the process of helping his son learn a new skill. And it was equally clear that Kyle felt truly accomplished at his newfound abilities.

As we watched this scene play out, we were amazed by Paul's restraint. We were just itching to demonstrate to Kyle how to do all this. "Just watch us," we thought, "and we'll show you how it's done." Yet it didn't even seem to occur to Paul to take the pole or the line from his son to demonstrate.

That was our epiphany. Recognize the student's talents and desires and treat him as the individual he is. Paul recognized Kyle's desire to excel, and he saw his role as a coach to merely guide Kyle to overcome his current skill barriers.

There were two things here that we loved about Paul as a coach. First, he recognized his son's natural abilities, including his great enthusiasm. Second, he guided Kyle in achieving his goals by coaching him rather than doing it for him or smothering him with directions. He allowed Kyle to learn and achieve in his own way.

So, is it always as straightforward as this? Just find a person who is struggling a bit, then do the horse whisperer routine to talk him or her onto a path to success? What about when there are several people involved, such as commonly happens with an established functional team or working group?

Highly successful managers sometimes make a seemingly illogical choice when it comes to assembling a high-performance team. They may actually choose people who don't, at least according to the resumes, appear to be the "very best."

They make this choice because sometimes those who appear to be the very best, as judged by their individual skills and abilities, don't play well with others. Such folks may be soloists, prima donnas, or just plain uncooperative. Whatever the reason, their inclusion in the group is not as beneficial as the inclusion of someone who appears less talented but who works very well with others in the group.

We see this commonly, of course, in more public team settings, such as athletics. The best team may be composed of "journeymen," "regulars," or "no-names." In the movie *Miracle*, which chronicled the gold medal success of the U.S. Olympic hockey team in 1980, the coach handed his list of desired players to his assistant. The stunned assistant said, "But you've left off some of the best players." "I don't want the best players," said the coach. "I want the best team."

So it is with your business. Sometimes the best combination of people includes someone who appears not to be the very best; they just help the group become the very best.

Here's Mike again, talking with one of his new hires, Tony. They're talking about how to create a high-functioning work team.

Mike's Company

"Well, Tony", asked Mike, "how did your week go? Learn anything new?"

Tony tells Mike about his progress that week, the camaraderie of the crew, and especially about one of the crew members with an outsized personality, Ari. Mike seems to love all this.

"Tony, I'm glad that you're fitting in so well. It sounds like you're working well with the rest of the crew. And obviously you've met Ari. He's quite a character, isn't he?"

"I'll say. He keeps everyone laughing, that's for sure, and he works hard."

"Ari is one of our top performers, but he has a real talent for looking on the bright side of things. He also has a talent for keeping everyone around him in a positive frame of mind.

"When we interviewed him, about four years ago, his references assured us that he had the carpentry skills we needed. But one of the main reasons we hired him was for his personality. We wanted someone who would do what he does: help to keep the crew upbeat and positive."

"So you mean that you hired him because he's a comedian?" Tony asked.

"No, we hired him because he had more than the minimum set of skills we needed and because he had abilities that others lacked. We knew that when we put him together with the other crew members that we'd get a hard working, upbeat group. He knew intuitively how to get others to have a good time while they were working. He was the missing ingredient at the time."

"The missing ingredient. What a strange way to think about a guy like Ari," said Tony.

"You seem a bit puzzled, Tony. Think of it this way. When you played in the school band, all the band members played a different instrument. In order to create the overall harmonious sound you wanted, you needed different people who would complement each other.

"In our company, we work hard to find people that will complement each other as a team. We don't want lots of the same kinds of folks. On our project crews, where work is intense and people work closely together, both physically and figuratively, we want to be sure that we have a positive atmosphere. For the crew you're on, Ari was our answer. And he's been great."

Tony had to admit, this made sense. Ari really was the guy that was most responsible for making the team so productive.

HIRE THE RIGHT PERSON, NOT THE RIGHT RESUME

The resume is a powerful document. It's been around for decades, and it shows little sign of disappearing any day soon. It's usually a candidate's first means of creating an impression with a desired organization, and many companies rely heavily upon it to create a picture of the candidates that apply to them.

Candidates go to great lengths to craft a resume that stands out, extorts their virtues, and seems to position them perfectly for the position they seek. There are books, Internet sites, and consultants that focus on helping candidates craft just the right tone, content, and format.

In turn, companies quickly screen out those candidates whose resumes don't show the right stuff. Then, they often look even harder at the remaining resumes to see if the candidates have already accomplished a similar position or if the details of the resume point to a fatal flaw.

You can see that a lot of calories are burned up in these activities by candidates as well as companies, all of whom take this document seriously. This would be fine, actually, if the resume were an accurate predictor for how well the candidate will perform in the position you seek to fill. Too often, however, that is not the case.

Now, don't get us wrong. We think that the resume can be a useful starting point for understanding a candidate's history and accomplishments (assuming the resume is truthful). We just want to caution you against taking it at face value. You need to look beyond the resume and discover for yourself the candidate's natural abilities that might or might not allow her to be successful in the position you are filling.

We can imagine you saying, "Of course I'll do that. I didn't fall off a turnip truck last week." And we hope that's true (that you'll do that, and that you didn't fall off a turnip truck last week). Unfortunately, we've seen too many managers fall into the trap of believing the resume is a predictor of success.

—————————————— A True Story ——————————————

We worked at a company that had recently hired a new president. He had a resume that shined. It described how he had accomplished almost everything desirable for someone seeking the President position, and he was hired.

It wasn't long, however, before his actual capabilities indicated that he was not the person for the position. He was running the company into the ground and quickly alienating a highly capable staff.

The CEO of the company asked his top managers for an evaluation of the president. He was concerned, and rightly so, about allowing this individual to continue in the position.

Although the CEO received a relatively consistent story about the president's lack of competence, one of the CEO's vice presidents had a different notion. "Well, I agree that he's not doing a good job right now, but he must be qualified," said the manager. "After all, he held a similar position in his former company."

So there it was. Despite direct observations that the president wasn't doing the job, a top manager of the company concluded that the president must be qualified because he previously held a similar position. This manager was so impressed with the president's resume that he couldn't interpret the data right in front of him.

So this must be a unique situation, right? No one else would come to such conclusions, would they?

If only that were true. This kind of thinking just takes different forms. The resume influences our thoughts and conclusions so strongly that sometimes it is difficult for people to be as skeptical as they should. Using the resume as their guide, they sometimes hire the person they imagine—the person that they want to believe can accomplish the position successfully.

A Client's Story

One of our clients was a prominent wholesale distributor of goods sold in retail stores. To better support their daily operations, they had developed a software program that greatly assisted them as well as their clients. Now they wanted to commercialize the software itself, something that clearly was outside their core expertise.

They began a search for someone to lead this new effort. They needed someone who could understand the target markets for the product, continue to develop the product to serve those markets, and then deliver a quality product to the customers.

The development effort itself was being undertaken by several current employees. It was a group of less than 10, and the atmosphere was common to many entrepreneurial ventures: Everyone pitched in to do whatever was needed. This was the culture that would greet the new manager.

The CEO and CFO obtained a resume of a fellow from out of state that they wanted to meet. In fact, they loved his resume. He was from a nationally recognized company, he held a modest though important-sounding title, and his resume outlined a long list of accomplishments at his current company.

The two executives flew the candidate in for a lunchtime interview. They were already convinced that they would be fortunate to land someone from this high-profile company to lead their software development effort. Now they had a chance to confirm their impressions.

Throughout the entire interview, the executives described their company, the software product and its development, and their needs for a new manager. They described the history of the company, the company benefits, and the advantages of working and living in their city.

They never asked the candidate a single question. They were salesmen on a mission: to convince this obviously qualified candidate to join their company.

He did. And he didn't work out.

There is one more issue related to the resume that you should consider: truthfulness. We suspect that people have embellished their resumes since the first one was written, but you want to be sure that you hire someone who is truthful (their words match the facts). You and your team will be working with this person, and you need to know that he can be trusted.

We caution you against believing that a lie on the resume is acceptable—that the person will be truthful to you in his new position, although he lied to get that position. We think this is delusional and that this untruthfulness is a key issue of principles. You can't afford it.

A True Story

We once interviewed a candidate for a senior sales position in a company that offered laboratory and industrial hygiene services. This position required a high level of technical skill, an ability to establish a good relationship with a client quickly, and careful attention to follow through to ensure that the client's needs were met. This was not an easy position to fill.

We interviewed a candidate whose resume was terrific. He had great experience at a similar company, presented himself very well, and was very knowledgeable about the services he would offer and the industry in general. He was perfect. We recommended hiring him, pending a background check.

Oops. It turned out that he didn't really have that college degree that was listed on his resume. Why not? Well, he said, he thought the resume would look better with that degree on it. He was sorry.

So were we. How could we ever trust this guy? What would be next? Would he lie about his expense report, or what the client really said to him, or who knows what?

We couldn't hire this candidate. And the degree actually meant nothing to us. We just wanted someone who could excel at the job. But we also wanted someone we could trust.

So, please continue to use the resume as the candidate's explanation of past achievements. Verify the facts, determine the candidate's skills and natural abilities, and assess the candidate's ability to work effectively in your environment.

However, even if it turns out that everything on the resume is true, remember the caveat tagged onto major financial offerings: "Past performance is no guarantee of future results." Your environment is different than the candidate's current environment, and those differences may be significant.

That's why understanding the candidate's underlying natural abilities is so important. You need to know if they have the tools to survive and excel in your environment.

Points to Remember

- We all can succeed if we're put in the right situation.

- We all can fail if we're put in the wrong situation.

- The job of owners and managers is to match the right people to the position and to coach those people to perform at a high level.

  - Define the position and its requirements.
  - Understand each person's natural abilities .
  - Find the right person—the person with the skills and natural abilities for the position.
  - Be clear about the goals.
  - Coach each person to excellence—understand how to extract his or her best.

- Hire the right person, not the right resume.

CHAPTER 4

Serve the right customer

---------------------- A True Story ----------------------

Long, long ago, in a place far away, one of us had a federal government client. This client was part of a fast-growing agency, but he was just one of many folks looking for a way to stand out from his colleagues.

We discussed an assignment with our client that required a great deal of research and analysis in an emerging area of governmental concern. No one had looked into these particular issues, and it was possible that our findings could have significant implications for a very small segment of the U.S. economy.

We took the assignment, and our team did an exhaustive job of research. We analyzed the data carefully to create some conclusions that would have a direct effect upon government regulations.

We explained our conclusions in a document that we submitted to our client, and we talked with him about our study. He liked what we had done and, after adding his own personal touches, he submitted the report to the head of his agency for review and approval.

To our surprise, our client received a significant cash reward for winning some version of the agency's "most important research" award. Bear in mind that the client received the award, not us, but we all knew that we helped make him shine with his superiors. We didn't go away empty-handed, however. Our reward was a "job well done" and the grant of additional work from the agency in the months following.

This story could be the introduction for a chapter on customer service. We could shower you with stories of exceptional service and urge you to create a culture that is customer-centric.

And indeed it is, at least in part, just that: a chapter on dealing effectively with your customers. But it is more than that, because we want you to actually design as well as conduct your operations with the customer in mind.

This may require a modification to the way that you now do business. More specifically, you may often think about ways to improve your operation, but do you define improvement in terms of your clients' needs or yours?

For example, you might create invoices in a format chosen by your bookkeeper rather than in a format that is understandable to your client (as was done by one of our former banks, emphasis on former). Or, you might package four widgets to a bundle, because that's the way you've always done it, even though the customer might need only three at a time.

A True Story

The Pike Place Market in Seattle is world famous for its vegetables, meats, and fish. And it surely must rank as one of the most interesting places in Seattle to watch people at work and play.

The market contains numerous open-air stalls, specialty shops, restaurants, and sidewalk entertainers. It's an ongoing, year-round festival of humanity and goods.

One day at the market, we visited one of the specialty grocers. This place simply has great products, some of them found nowhere else in Seattle. It's difficult to walk through the aisles without maintaining a constant bug-eyed expression.

After exceeding our original budget two times over, we proceeded to the check-out area. Here's where the real fun began.

After ringing up our purchases, the woman at the check-out register told us the total. We handed her a credit card for the payment, just like we had done successfully on all our previous visits here.

She nodded at a small black device mounted on a pedestal at the side of the check-out counter. It was one of the now-ubiquitous card readers, all of which seem to require that the card's magnetic strip be on the side opposite to the one first chosen.

I asked her politely why the store had moved to this new system.

"It's easier," she replied.

"Oh," I replied, "I liked it better when you swiped the card. That seemed pretty easy."

"Not really," she replied, still not even cracking a smile.

Perhaps it was easier for them. It certainly wasn't easier or quicker for me.

I watched other people go through the line, and it was clear that the card-swiping activity took two or three times as long as done by a check-out person. Everyone seemed to have my handicap: an inability to quickly figure out which edge of the card should face the machine and whether the card should face up or face down.

Our check out person obviously didn't have a clue about her customers' true needs. In fact, we doubt that she'd even consider them to be her customers; that would imply a type of ownership.

On the other hand, if she had been a customer advocate, she might have tried to make the check-out experience an easy one, not an exercise on how to be baffled. Or, at the very least, she might have brought some empathy and good cheer to the conversation. But she was poorly trained, and the store missed an opportunity to impress a customer and earn loyalty.

Building your company around your customers requires you to think quite differently than the cashier in the Pike Place Market. It requires you to consider your customers as the architects of your business, and consequently compels you to design your entire firm to serve those customers.

This is a lesson learned by virtually all *successful* sole proprietors. Without a group of multi-skilled and multi-functional coworkers, the successful sole proprietor focuses on a specific segment of the market and learns how to serve that market in an exemplary way. Thus, the successful sole proprietor (who also is the entire company) adopts procedures and habits that are designed to serve customers in such a way as to ensure the proprietor's success.

This notion is oftentimes lost in larger firms. Once we move from the successful sole proprietorship to a larger firm, we find processes that may be implemented for internal benefits, managers that may focus on the growth of their own empires, and employees that focus only on the easiest means of completing their particular jobs. The customer may be virtually forgotten, at least as a focal point.

We all know that we need customers, and we all know that we have to serve the customer in some good way. But how many of us structure our company in the best interest of the customer? Don't we often structure things to be convenient for us, and hope that it works out okay for the customer? Is okay good enough?

We urge you to consider a modification in the way that you do business. Depending upon your current status, this could mean only minor variations to your current structure and processes or, alternatively, something much more significant.

There are five steps, or building blocks, for building your company around your customers. All of these steps can be accomplished by virtually any business.

- Define the right customers.
- Create the right strategies for your right customers.
- Create a sales process to secure and serve your right customers.
- Create an operations process to serve your right customers.
- Constantly build the culture.

DEFINE THE RIGHT CUSTOMERS

One of the most valuable questions to ask about your business is "What defines the right customers for us?" The answer will vary from business to business, so there is no common list of attributes that you can borrow with confidence. But if you take the time to really think about this question, you should be able to create a list of characteristics that describe your ideal, or nearly ideal, customers.

Generally, this exercise asks you to match your vision and capabilities with the needs and wants of your potential customers. It also requires you to come to terms with the notion that there are some folks who just shouldn't be your customers.

There are many good reasons for this. Two of the most common include the fact that your company simply may not be equipped to serve some particular customers to their satisfaction and that some customers may make demands upon your firm that are unreasonably onerous.

Some businesses ignore their own inability to serve particular customers to their satisfaction. They continue to work hard, committing to new client engagements, and continuing to fall short in delighting the customer and in generating profitable return business.

There are many firms, however, that recognize early that cultivating the right customer is good both for them and for the customer. And they also learn, and indeed are happy, to let another firm serve those who are not "the right customers" for them.

For example, a well-known discount clothing chain uses this phrase as its tag line: "An educated consumer is our best customer." This phrase is both flattering and discerning. When we shop at this chain, we like to think that we are indeed an educated consumer and not just another casual shopper. On the other hand, the tag line and the stores themselves also tell us that we'd better be educated, because we won't get a lot of service here. This is a place for bargain hunters who know what they want and are willing to spend the time to find it, without the help of highly trained customer-focused store personnel.

Some customers may also be undesirable because they make unreasonable demands upon your firm. These demands may be intentional or not, but the results are the same: You are unable to transact business to either satisfy the customer or to generate a reasonable profit.

Oftentimes we define the right customer as one that gives us lots of sales. In most businesses, it is common to find that a large proportion of the sales (for example, 80 percent) are obtained from a small proportion of the customers (for example, 20 percent). This is the so-called 80/20 Rule, which is often used to identify our major customers, the ones that we frequently refer to as our "good customers."

The converse interpretation of the 80/20 Rule, of course, is that a majority of our customers (for example, 80 percent) may account for only a relatively small proportion of sales (for example, 20 percent). At first blush, then, it seems logical to think of these folks as our "small customers," and to conclude that they are of lesser importance than the "big boys."

Unfortunately for those of us who seek simplicity, this may or may not be true. For example, we might have a big client, accounting for a large proportion of our sales, who makes enough demands upon us that we actually lose money, or make very little, on their transactions.

Similarly, a too-small customer may not be a good one if the costs required to process a sale leads to low profitability (transaction costs are too high). Conversely, that same "too-small" customer may be a good one if that small initial order will lead to a long-term profitable relationship, or if we can determine how to lower the transaction costs.

These examples only further illustrate the value of defining the right customer. Remember that the characteristics of the right customer are specific to your firm—you'll need to think carefully about the attributes that you value in your customers.

Here's an example. We haven't talked with the discount clothing firm we referenced previously, but we might guess at the characteristics for their right customers. Here they are:

- Frequent clothes buyer.
- Likes shopping for bargains (price is an important issue).
- Likes to browse/shop without a salesperson (confident of what they want).
- Needs minimal alterations (fits the standard sizes).
- Likes brand-name clothes (especially if inexpensive).
- Unconcerned about store ambiance (Why should I pay for marble floors?).
- Willing to return multiple times to find the right thing (It's like a treasure hunt).

The staffing implications for this retail clothier are fairly obvious. They don't need a team of old-world tailors and gentlemanly salespeople with decades of fine clothing experience. They need a competent tailor, some savvy purchasing managers to find those bargain clothes, and some fast-working floor clerks and warehouse folks to keep the merchandise moving. This results in a decades-long business that satisfies a distinct segment of the market.

Now let's contrast those characteristics with a firm that supplies critical-function computer services to other businesses. The list of right customer characteristics might include:

- Depends upon us for quick response to problems.
- Appreciates our high-quality products and services.
- Willing to pay premium prices (price is not an issue).
- Wants guidance and consultation on services.

- Appreciates our frequent maintenance visits.
- Likes having a strong relationship with us.
- Loyal—unwilling to shop around if receiving good service.

The staffing implications for this firm are significantly different than for the clothier. This firm needs highly skilled technical people who can act as trusted advocates for the success of the customers. The staff must be customer-focused and able to deliver complex solutions in a short time. They need to be skilled communicators and strong relationship builders. This results in a business that can charge premium fees and assemble a growing list of loyal customers.

Obviously, you should define your right customers carefully. That will allow you to create the right strategies and processes to acquire and satisfy those customers. These include the ways in which you identify and target those customers, as well as the ways in which you sell to them and operate your day-to-day business to satisfy and delight them.

CREATE THE RIGHT STRATEGIES FOR YOUR RIGHT CUSTOMERS

Once you've determined what your right customers look like, the next step is to create strategies to acquire those customers. This is, of course, part of the process of planning, discussed earlier, and it now carries an even more specific focus. Now you'll be determining the specific steps and actions you'll take that will win over your client prospects and engage them as good customers.

Strategies can be separated into two types: generic and specific. The generic strategy is based upon the premise that truly successful and outstanding companies must excel as one of three generic types:

1. The low-cost leader.
2. Differentiated by exceptional customer service.
3. Differentiated by exceptional products or services.

The specific strategies describe in clear detail how these generic strategies will be implemented in your company.

Generic strategies

We've had countless discussions with business owners and managers through the years about the generic strategies that they employ. Do they try to offer the lowest prices? Or do they try to differentiate themselves by offering exemplary service or outstanding products?

Many times these managers have acted surprised at these questions. In our business, they say, we have to give the customer all three. That's what they want.

This is actually a difficult discussion for many owners and managers, and it may be for you also. You may feel like many business owners and managers: You have lots of competitive pressure in your business and you're probably trying to find customers wherever and whenever you can. You want to keep as many folks happy as possible, so you try to give them what they want (the lowest prices, the best service, the best products).

Unfortunately, this is virtually an impossible task. The companies that excel as being low cost providers, customer focused, or exemplary product leaders have widely varying characteristics, as we'll discuss, including:

- **The nature of the customers.**
- **The degree of standardization in day-to-day operations.**
- **Focus on buying power.**
- **Focus on innovation.**
- **The degree of autonomy for employees.**
- **The degree of centralized management.**

Following is a diagram that illustrates the process of choosing a generic strategy. Here's how we think about this. If you can successfully distinguish your organization through great service or products, you should be able to charge prices that allow you to be profitable. If you can't distinguish your organization, or if you choose to be the low-cost provider (such as Costco or Wal-Mart), you'll need to operate very efficiently in order to offer low prices and still make a profit.

Choosing a Generic Strategy

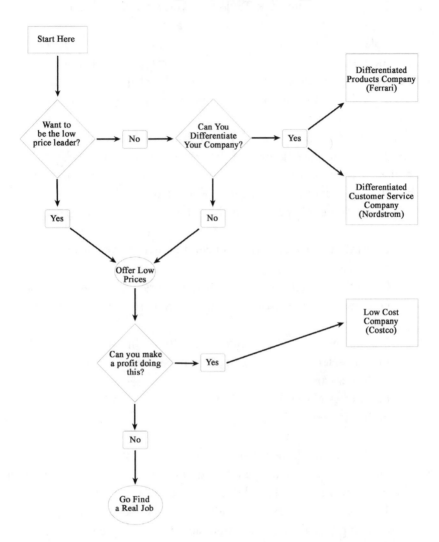

Low cost

Being a company that offers a low price (the price tag to the customer) is rather easy—at least for a short while. You can drop your prices to very low levels anytime you'd like. If you do it to clear out slow-moving merchandise, you might call it a clearance sale. If you try to do this indefinitely, it might be financial suicide. The real trick of a low-cost company, then, is to offer low prices indefinitely, still make a profit, and keep doing it over and over again, day after day. To do this, you must first obtain your own products or services at low cost (the price tag to you).

People frequently think of Wal-Mart or Costco as low-cost companies. And indeed they are—they have enormous purchasing power, which they use to negotiate low-cost products from their suppliers (whether these firms can consistently and profitably offer low-cost products to Wal-Mart is another story).

Low-cost firms have a few things in common. We've already seen one of them: large purchasing power, which is needed to obtain products from suppliers at consistently low costs. A small firm, lacking such purchasing power, typically cannot obtain goods at these low costs.

Here are some other common characteristics of low-cost firms:

- **Operations are standardized (avoiding expensive customized activities).**
- **Operations are focused on avoiding errors (errors cost money).**
- **Operations are measured and managed carefully (to increase efficiency).**
- **Management is strongly centralized (to maintain consistency).**
- **Products/services are aimed at the mass market (most of the customers are here).**
- **Employees have very clear jobs, goals, and boundaries (to maintain control).**

The irony here is that lowering prices is easy, while making a profit is not. Company owners and managers very frequently lower their prices when seeking to grow their firms, and this often works. They get more sales. The difficult thing to do is to get more sales and still make a profit.

For example, it is virtually impossible for a relatively small firm to acquire the purchasing power of a very large firm. (Joining a co-op or buying group may help reduce costs, although the costs generally are the same for all similar-sized co-op members.) Thus, the costs incurred by the small firm will make it more difficult for the firm to make a profit, relative to a large firm, if the small firm tries to sell its goods at the same price.

Additionally, it requires significant dedication and focus to create the processes, discipline, and culture to drive down costs relentlessly. In fact, virtually every dimension of the firm must reflect this generic low-cost strategy if it is to be successful.

The centralized management team must standardize operations to drive down day-to-day costs and avoid errors that add to costs. They must closely manage the employees to ensure that they do exactly what is expected, and they must constantly measure and manage the details of the operations to gain incremental improvements through time. They also must choose the firm's customers carefully, focusing on those who are not highly demanding, but rather are happy with the firm's existing offerings (no custom stuff).

This low-cost firm is, overall, a very tightly and centrally managed operation, with the people to match the culture. Like the Olympic high jump, not everyone can do it. But we know that some can, and we know that they can become very successful.

Differentiated products and services

A second generic strategy is to offer products (we'll use the word *products* here to represent both products and professional services) that stand out from those offered by other companies. If these standout products are truly valued by customers, the firm won't have to resort to low prices to sell them.

There are many examples of this across all industries. Products such as BMW automobiles, Calvin Klein jeans, and Apple products are all sold to consumers who value some intrinsic quality or perceived benefit in the product. And they are willing to pay a premium price to obtain them.

In some cases, the prices that customers will pay are almost breathtaking. Some golf clubs, for example, have an initiation fee of more than $100,000 and an annual fee of $25,000. That certainly keeps out the riff raff—creating a truly distinctive air of exclusivity.

So, what does the customer get for all this dough? Are these products really worth it?

The answer, of course, is that these products are worth it to the people (the right customers) that are delighted to pay for them. The tough part is to determine how to find and convince these particular people to pay these high fees. This is where the specific strategies, discussed here, play a role.

The key here is to find at least one way to differentiate the product in a meaningfully—a way that is valued by the customer. For example, many customers buy a BMW because they are convinced that their vehicle is the best handling car on the road, many people buy Calvin Klein jeans because of the status conferred by wearing designer clothing, and many people buy Apple products because they are stylish and technologically advanced, and when other people see your new Apple i-something, they say, "Oh, wow!"

It's important to note that the customer's perceptions are more important than "actual facts." For example, we know that an inexpensive electronic watch keeps time as well or better than an ultra high-end mechanical "chronograph" watch, despite all the descriptive hype about how well the watch is constructed. That's immaterial. People don't buy that fancy watch just to keep time—it's an icon of success.

The customer's perception of the product—the "position" that the product holds in the customer's mind—is of utmost importance in determining how well the product is distinguished. The firm simply must find a way to position its product as an outstanding one.

A firm can certainly do this with "the facts." Indeed, BMW has pages of test data and an endless stream of advertising to convince us that their cars truly are exceptional performers. Similarly, there are products in virtually all fields that can demonstrate their superiority with data.

Even for firms with the information to demonstrate their product superiority, there is still work to do. It is simply not enough to trot out the data. Customers need to be convinced. There are many tales of superior products that did not catch on with customers as well as the facts might have led us to predict (Sony Betamax, Apple computer software). But even when we have "the facts," we must remember that it is the customer who places a value on those facts. So, we must have specific strategies to determine how to convince the customer of our products' value.

Honda is the world's leading automobile engine manufacturer. They might have simply tried to convince people of this through repetitive fact-based advertising, as they sometimes do. They have also done other things, however, that are strategically designed to position the firm, in the customers' mind, as the world's leading engine maker. For example, they manufacture engines for a wide variety of applications (for example, automobiles, lawnmowers, motorcycles, generators), they have participated in a high-profile racing program designed to showcase their technology and success, and they continually tout the cutting-edge technologies embodied in their engines (ultra-low emission engines, hybrid engines, and so forth).

Alternatively, some firms can differentiate their products by ignoring the facts, while finding some other means of convincing us of some important benefits. These firms recognize that there are many factors that influence buyers' decisions. In effect, the "facts" may not even be important to some customers.

Let's look at designer jeans as an example. Is the denim really better, stronger, tougher, more supple? Is the stitching more robust, the zippers zippier? Even if that were the case, the designers don't even discuss it in their advertising. Instead, they position their product as one that is worn by the hip, the beautiful, and the knowing. We buy this stuff because it's cool, and we are happy to pay the price.

Similarly, objective tests run by a nationally known consumer testing organization concluded that New York City water was of the highest quality and was preferred to "designer water" by tasters in blind tasting tests (that is, they didn't know which water they were drinking). Nevertheless, consumers are willing to spend billions of dollars to drink bottled waters from exotic glaciers and mysterious wells, and they do this because they perceive some benefit from it (taste, status, perceived health benefits, holding a cool-looking bottle).

The firms that successfully differentiate their products have some characteristics that are quite distinctive, and certainly different from those of a low-cost company. Here are a few:

- The products are constantly being improved or replaced with better ones.
- Customers anticipate and desire the new stand-out products.
- Customers are willing to pay a premium for such products.
- The company culture values creativity and tomorrow's ideas.
- Employees enjoy the challenge of creating the next best thing.
- Management is willing to take calculated risks.
- Management is not rigid, but basic rules are followed.
- The firm can quickly change direction; it's highly flexible.

The successful firm that differentiates itself by its products is run by managers who value new ideas and new ways to satisfy customers. The employees love to get up in the morning if it means that they can work on creative new products and be challenged to produce things that haven't been seen before. And the firm satisfies its customers when it delivers stand-out products, even if they are high priced.

These firms create new products that out-compete their old products, and they do this before the competition does it. For many years Intel did this with its ever-improved line of computer chips, and Apple continues to wow its customers with exceptional and creative products every year.

Notice also that management in a product-differentiated company is not focused on standardizing operations as it is in a low-cost company. Innovation is the coin of the realm, and the company is very willing to spend money on tinkering and experiments. Such a company does not put cost cutting at the focus of its day-to-day operations.

Differentiated customer service

The third generic strategy is to offer outstanding customer service. If the level of service offered by the firm is truly valued by customers, the firm won't have to resort to low prices to sell its products.

—————————————— **A True Story** ——————————————

One of our wives is an avid bicycle rider. Some days she rides 60 to 100 miles—and she calls it fun. She even smiles while she's doing it.

She purchased her newest bike from a shop that provides lifetime service (adjust the brakes, the gear shifts, the chain). One afternoon, after washing off her bike after a long ride, she left it at the corner of the garage, right behind our automobile. When we backed out to do an errand, we also ran over the rear wheel of the bike.

The bike shop fixed the wheel at no charge. This certainly wasn't part of the lifetime service, at least not in our mind, but they invested a few minutes time to keep a good customer happy. They didn't even push us to buy a new wheel, though we surely would have done so.

Their customer, however, is a vocal billboard for the shop. Just ask her where to buy a bike.

One of the questions we always ask business owners is "What makes your company special?" The answer that we hear, without fail, is "our people." This reminds us of the radio show "Prairie Home Companion," where "all the children are above average."

There are numerous firms that say that they are customer-friendly, customer-intimate, or customer oriented. Regardless of the term, they want to believe it—just as much as they want to believe that their people are special.

It requires real dedication and focus, however, to truly stand out in this regard. In today's marketplaces, the level of customer service is constantly being raised. So, it is ever more difficult to distinguish a firm in this regard.

For those who can do so, however, it provides a truly distinctive and long-lasting means for creating customer loyalty. And for many of us, the price we pay for distinctive service is well worth it.

A True Story

One of us (the other guy) loves to wear fine clothing. He loves to look at it, purchase it, and show it off—and it simply makes him feel good to wear it.

At one time, he frequented a specialty men's shop where the service was exemplary (in another state from his current residence, unfortunately). The salesman was a long time employee who took a personal interest in all his clients' preferences, and he made extraordinary efforts to know, understand, and delight his clients.

Quite commonly, he would call when something of potential interest arrived at the shop. He'd pick out a tie that matched well with the newly arrived shirt, and then he'd drape a great suit over it all, virtually compelling his customer to purchase the entire ensemble.

My coauthor spent a fortune in that place through the years—purchasing countless things that he didn't even know he needed. And he loved every minute of it!

Bear in mind that the shop mentioned previously didn't have anything that was truly unique. The same shirts and ties could be purchased elsewhere. It was simply the level of service—in this case the truly personal touch—that compelled customers to shop there.

At firms such as this, customers buy because of the relationships forged by the people in these firms. These companies actually do have people that are special—people who love to delight their customers by meeting and anticipating their needs and wants.

There are many ways to delight customers, but we find at least two major ways that firms can distinguish themselves in this regard, regardless of industry: to save the customer time or to help the customer avoid stress.

Our culture places a high value on time: Any way that we can save time for a customer is a potential opportunity to provide highly-valued service. The importance of this concept became obvious to us years ago when we read the results of a consumer survey. The survey reminded folks that they should drink eight glasses of water each day for their health. It then asked people why they didn't do so. The single most prominent reason given for not drinking eight glasses of water each day was "Not enough time"!

It was clear to us from this survey that consumers' perceptions about time were powerful enough to over-ride logic. Surely, we all have enough time to drink water, but we have somehow convinced ourselves that we don't.

The tailor shop we described helped customers save time. They didn't have to shop around (takes too much time), or come back on numerous occasions to find the right shirt (takes too much time), or repeatedly try to match ties with shirts (takes way too much time).

Helping customers avoid stress is a second major way to distinguish ourselves in customer service, regardless of industry. Once again, when customers realize that you've helped relieve their stress, you have opened an opportunity for a distinctive relationship.

A True Story

One of those "big box" handyman stores recently had a sale of barbeque grills. They gave the customer two choices: buy it for $129 all boxed up or $139 fully assembled.

The last time we tried to put one of these things together, we had parts and screws left over and it took a good part of the morning. When we were done, we'd been stressed to a level not appreciated by our spouse.

We paid the extra $10 for preassembly and smiled for the rest of the day.

The firms that successfully differentiate themselves through exceptional customer service have distinctive characteristics in common. Here are a few:

- They focus on how to improve customers lives.
- Their knowledge and expertise are their strengths (not products).
- They are happy to have a select group of customers.
- Customers want the best solution for *them*—not necessarily "the best."
- Customers are willing to pay a premium for such services.
- The culture is driven by the client.
- Employees are empowered to delight the customer.
- Employees build relationships with customers for the long term.

A True Story

One of us recently received a nasty computer virus, something the creative folks call a Trojan Horse. This is an insidious software infection that slows down the computer and opens the door for other viruses to enter, leaving the computer vulnerable to continuous bombardment by advertisers or even the destruction of data.

We obtained instructions for removing this Trojan Horse from a very reputable software firm. They even indicated that it was not difficult to perform this feat.

Nevertheless, we remain skeptics when it comes to the magic of pixels, binary code, and software programs. It's all blue smoke and mirrors to us, and we get nervous just thinking about the consequences of hitting the wrong key. Our stress was peaking.

We decided to call in an expert. Our initial thought was one of relief: We were delighted to allow someone else to assume our complex problem. We were happy to pay him—freeing us from the stress of dealing with frustrating error messages, exacting instructions, and commands to perform obtuse operations and then to "restart your computer."

As it turned out, the computer had 93 separate infections and it required four hours of our expert's time to fix it. We watched him part of the time, and were amazed at his dexterity: His fingers flew across the keyboard, opening screens that we'd never seen before. How would we have possibly done this on our own? Why would we even want to try?

We still glow in the aftermath of this virtuoso's performance. We didn't do a thing except write a check to a person who helped us avoid a day's worth of frustration. What a bargain!

All three simultaneously

What if a company decides to attempt to provide all three generic strategies—low prices, great customer service, and great products? Can a company excel by doing this?

This was the situation we described at the beginning of this chapter, the one that many business owners feel compelled to pursue. After all, doesn't the customer want all three? Why can't you be the one to give them all three?

There are significant barriers in attempting to practice all three generic strategies, because each of them requires that the firm exhibit specific characteristics, many of which are "mutually exclusive." That is, the characteristics required to excel in one of the strategies may be highly disadvantageous for another of the strategies.

For example, firms that are differentiated by their products excel because of a cadre of managers and staff who embrace change are willing to take risks, and are constantly looking to do things differently than before. This is in stark contrast to the low-cost firms that revere routine, work hard to eliminate risks, and abhor custom work or doing things differently than they have done yesterday or last month

Similarly, the staff and management at a customer focused company are constantly thinking of ways to delight their customers, and these customers are, by definition, folks who value highly the attention they receive. Thus, the company spends time and money on new and innovative ways to bring specific benefits to these customers. This again is in contrast to low-cost firms that hire managers and staff who are focused on value-oriented customers who are willing to forego fancy service in order to save money.

Despite their inherent differences, however, there are basic levels of competence firms must possess in all three generic strategies. The product-differentiated company must still operate efficiently or it won't make a profit, and the low-cost company must still have reasonably good products or customers won't buy them. And both of these firms must have an acceptable level of customer service.

The message here is that to truly excel, firms must choose and perfect one of the three generic strategies. To do otherwise is to invite operational conflict, managerial schizophrenia, employee confusion, and low profits. In other words, you'll be just another average company or worse.

Specific strategies

Once your company has committed to one of the three generic strategies, you must create more detailed strategies that are specific to your business. These specific strategies describe in detail the activities your company will accomplish to reach its goals, all within the framework of its generic strategy.

Here's an example, from a product-differentiated firm that builds seats for kayaks: small, one-person boats used on white-water rivers. The brief description here illustrates some specific strategies that will allow the firm to execute on its generic strategy, which is to be the product-differentiated firm in the industry.

A Kayak Seat Builder

In order to implement our Generic Strategy of Product Leadership, it is important that we understand the characteristics of our customers. Our strategies should be focused on those characteristics and how we can best satisfy our customers with the cutting-edge products they desire.

Our customers (white-water kayak manufacturers) are populated with relatively young (20- to 35-year-old) employees and managers who are risk-takers, open to changes in design and construction, and very demanding of quick responses to their requests for new designs. Consequently, we will continue to hire and train our salespeople to be responsive to these needs and to work closely with our production staff to implement the new designs requested by our clients.

In the future, we will take some new steps to increase our market share in this segment. For the white-water niche in which we participate, we will conduct several activities to raise our awareness with manufacturers that we are a cutting-edge seat designer.

- First, we will only hire salespeople who are themselves kayakers, and thus understand implicitly the needs of the manufacturer and the end user.

- Second, we will sponsor at least three national races as well as two world-class kayakers, and we will advertise our products on the boats of these two competitors.

- Third, we will train our salespeople to help design and promote the newest cutting-edge designs and colors, and we will confer a "Cutting-Edge Award" each year to the innovator of the best-selling new product.

- Fourth, our design team will meet quarterly with our key accounts to discuss new products, potential new designs and colors, and special needs for integrating our product in the manufacturing process."

You can see that these strategies are focused on the design and promotion of new products. Though there is an element of customer service ("…meet quarterly with key accounts…"), this clearly is a firm that reveres its creative development skills. It's focused on creating superior products.

You'll need to do something similar for your own firm. Construct specific and detailed strategies, within your generic strategy, that will compel you to achieve your goals. You can't steal these strategies from someone else; they're specific to your company.

As we discussed previously, these strategies will change through time. And that is why you should use the Spider Diagram regularly to keep everyone tuned in to the marketplace—to assess the need for updating the strategies. And that will make the company's strategies clear and relevant to everyone.

CREATE A SALES PROCESS TO SECURE AND SERVE YOUR RIGHT CUSTOMERS

Once you have described your right customers, and created generic and specific strategies to achieve success, you must create a sales process for actually securing those customers. Please note, though, that these are not really sequential steps; all of these activities are accomplished in an interactive way.

For example, when you define the right customers, you might consider the effort necessary to secure those customers—length of the sales cycle, cost, proximity to your people, and so forth. So these first three steps are activities that should be conducted together.

Elite sales-driven companies use a sales process to track their sales activities at every stage—from the first contact with a potential customer until the final delivery of the product. The process can be a complex one with multiple steps, but it really is comprised of two major activities: identifying prospective customers (generating leads) and compelling those prospective customers to buy (closing). Thus, we speak frequently of "lead generation" and "closing" as the two key activities in the sales process.

The sales funnel

In order to focus your activities on the specific actions needed to increase lead generation and improve closing, you should track your potential customers at several stages. Though some companies use 10 to 12 categories for this process, we'll illustrate the concept here with three, which is enough for many firms.

As a first step, let's look first at the overall picture for generating sales in a firm. This is depicted in the following Sales Funnel diagram:

The Sales Funnel

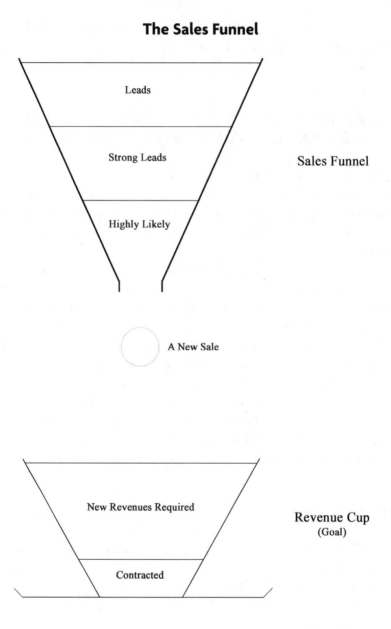

Leads

Strong Leads

Sales Funnel

Highly Likely

A New Sale

New Revenues Required

Revenue Cup
(Goal)

Contracted

The diagram shows that you are going to manage a process to attain a specified level of revenue for the coming time period—say, next year. This is represented by the cup, which holds the desired quantity of revenue.

In our diagram, the cup already contains some "contracted" revenue. This applies to companies that obtain work to be delivered and invoiced at some time in the future. For example, you might sign a contract (make a sale) to build a $30 million structure over three years, and you will receive $10 million in revenue each year, as progress is made. Such companies can get a "head start" on meeting their revenue targets for the coming year.

Note that for some businesses, such as this building contractor, the distinction between sales and revenues is important. The company might make a big sale today that covers multiple years of work, but it is only able to recognize the revenue in increments, as the work is completed. Other businesses, such as retailers, lack this distinction. They make sales and collect the money at the same time, and they do not have any contracted revenue for the coming year.

Regardless of whether your organization has contracted revenues or not, your job is to keep the funnel full of leads, and to close enough of them, with the right customers, to meet your revenue target. The sales funnel represents all the potential customers for your firm, from the earliest contacts to those that are about to purchase from you. You will monitor and manage the interactions with these potential customers to ensure that you choose the right customers in order to meet your targets. Here are the three major categories of potential customers in the funnel in our example here:

• Lead

This is a potential customer you believe can use your products. You now have to qualify the potential customer (for example, are they one of your right customers, do they have the funds, can you meet their needs, and so forth). Depending upon the industry, the time from identifying a lead to securing a sale can be measured in minutes (retail) to years (for example, certain professional services and big-ticket items).

Your focus here is to generate a continuous flow of leads. Because the probability of securing a sale from any specific lead usually is relatively low (often less than 20 percent, and sometimes much less), you'll need to have plenty of high-quality leads to hit your sales and revenue targets. Over time, you should be able to quantify the number of leads you need, on average, to generate a certain level of sales.

• **Strong Lead**

This is a potential customer that you now have qualified. This buyer needs your products, and has the money and the authority to buy from you. You know that it will still require a real concerted effort to make the sale.

Your focus here is to identify the activities required to distinguish your firm in light of the buyer's needs, because there are likely to be some specific actions that will need to be accomplished to win this sale. The probability of winning a sale may be in the 25 to 85 percent range (this broad range is a rationale for some firms to sub-divide this category into several others).

• **Highly Likely**

Potential customers in this category have indicated very strongly that you have an excellent chance to win the sale. The probability of this happening is in the range of 85 percent or greater. You have demonstrated your capabilities and benefits to the buyer, and you've gotten strong positive signals that this sale is ready to close.

Your focus is indeed just that: What must you do to close this sale and meet this client's needs? This is not the time to just "wait and see" but rather to be proactive in closing the sale.

Potential customers enter your Sales Funnel at the top as leads, and they exit the bottom as a new sale, dropping into the revenue cup to help fulfill your revenue target. As the probability of obtaining a signed contract or sale increases, the potential customer moves closer to the bottom exit of the funnel.

You know that all of your leads do not result in sales. So, your firm must ensure that it generates enough leads to result in sales that will meet its targets for the year. This is an important part of the overall sales process—generating a sufficient number of leads to meet your sales and revenue targets.

You also know that all the highly likely sales will not, in fact, result in a sale. For various reasons, and your company should understand them, you will lose a few. So, you must train your people on the most effective means for getting customers to actually make the purchase—for closing the sale.

The sales process

These two activities, lead generation and closing, are the heart of the sales process. The leads and strong leads categories focus the company on generating leads, listening to the customer to understand needs, and qualifying the prospective customer. The highly likely category focuses the company on activities needed to close the sale, such as convincing the customer that you can provide compelling benefits.

The sales process for your company should address both of these activities in detail. In fact, many firms have thoughtful ongoing sales training programs for both these activities.

In order to manage the overall sales process, you should track your prospective customers by each of the categories in the sales funnel. At a minimum, you should monitor the number of customers in each category, the sales dollars for each category (if available), and the probability of securing the sale for each of the prospective customers (especially important for the highly likely category). You also should create specific plans to move potential customers along the funnel to become actual customers.

The sales process for your firm should be a structured series of activities undertaken to maximize sales to your target customers. It should be based on the best sales practices for your firm, and consequently the process itself will be virtually unique to your firm. For example, a telemarketing firm will have an entirely different sales process than an engineering firm.

There are, however, some generic activities that can be applied to your firm. Because the sales process should be a structured series of activities, the first step in creating the process is to describe these major activities. Then, you should provide exacting detail and training for each step so that everyone uses the firm's best practices.

Your firm's selling activities can perhaps best be represented as a flow chart, an example of which is shown on page 134. Starting with the initial contact with a potential customer, the firm will identify each step in the selling process and then provide details on how each step should be conducted.

Example Sales Process

```
┌────────┐
│ Start  │
│ Here   │
└────────┘
    │
    ▼
┌──────────────┐      ┌──────────────┐      ┌──────────────┐      ┌──────────────┐
│Identify Correct│    │ First Phone  │      │ First Meeting│      │Second Meeting│
│Contact Person │ ──▶ │   Contact    │ ──▶  │(Client Needs,│ ──▶  │(Send Proposal)│
│              │      │ (Set Meeting)│      │ Our Benefits)│      │              │
└──────────────┘      └──────────────┘      └──────────────┘      └──────────────┘
                                                                          │
                                                                          ▼
┌────────┐      ◇ Selected as ◇      ┌──────────┐            ◇ Selected as ◇
│  Yes!  │ ◀──  ◇   winner?   ◇ ◀──  │  Submit  │ ◀── Yes ◀──◇ a Finalist? ◇
└────────┘      ◇            ◇        │Final Bid │            ◇            ◇
                     │               └──────────┘                 │
                     ▼                                            ▼
                  ┌────┐                                       ┌────┐
                  │ No │                                       │ No │
                  └────┘                                       └────┘
                     │          ┌──────────────┐                 │
                     └────────▶ │  Learn Why   │ ◀───────────────┘
                                │  We Were     │
                                │ Not Selected │
                                └──────────────┘
```

Let's assume that you have generated a lead (the name of a potential customer). You might view the first step in your sales process as an initial contact with this person.

Rather than simply call the person and "wing it," however, you decide to plan this call carefully in order to make your best introduction and first impression. In fact, you'd want everyone in the firm to use this same approach in other first calls with your prospects. We've provided an example for this first phone contact in Appendix D.

The previous diagram and the information on a first phone contact are only examples, and they most likely will not be directly applicable to your firm. You likely will need to modify these examples to your own situation, and through time you should continually search for and use the best practices for each step.

To make the process complete, of course, requires that you use this approach for every step of the process. And this goes way beyond mere mechanics. You should constantly search for effective ways to improve each step of the process.

For example, we've mentioned using your "best introduction." The idea here is that through time you have tried different introductions, paid close attention to customers' reactions, and created the best introduction you know. You've chosen your words and phrases with care in order to serve your target customers in a highly effective way.

This approach never ends; you continually refine each step of the sales process when you learn something more effective. And that is a real plus of using a system: Everyone knows and uses best practices and tries to improve upon them continually, so everyone on the team can benefit from everyone's experience and expertise.

In order to improve upon current practices, people must be allowed to try new things. In effect, you allow your folks to experiment with the steps in the sales process, adopting ideas that work better than the old ones.

One way to determine the effectiveness of your experiments is to measure results frequently. The objective, of course, is to improve the sales funnel, to generate more leads in the beginning, and to bring more of those leads to final sale.

Furthermore, you can measure your results at each stage of the sales funnel. If the company is declining in its ability to bring strong leads to highly likely, you probably will need to modify the procedures being used by your sales people in those steps.

In essence, the sales process is a trial-and-error development process. But the process is based upon the collective best practices of everyone in the group. And everyone in the group uses the best ideas available.

CREATE AN OPERATIONS PROCESS TO SERVE YOUR RIGHT CUSTOMERS

Once you have described your right customers, created generic and specific strategies to achieve success, and designed a sales process to acquire those right customers, you will turn to the internal day-to-day operations. Your objective here is to design your operations to best serve your right customers.

Although this seems like an obvious objective, the operations of many firms have evolved into a basket of activities that spring from bureaucracy, internal convenience, and habit. The customer has simply been left out of the design process.

The operations process is somewhat similar in concept to the sales process. It is a collection of best practices. But in this case it is a collection of practices that best allow you to serve the right customer in the delivery of your product or service.

For example, let's assume that you strive to be a low-cost company. Your objective is to continually drive down your own costs so that you can offer low prices to your customers—customers who highly value those low prices. If you were a retailer, you might encourage customers to bag their own purchases, saving costly labor for baggers. Then you'd position that activity positively by informing the customer of their cost savings through a modest bit of work.

Conversely, let's assume that you strive to be a company differentiated by customer service. Your objective is to truly stand out, not merely be an also-ran. If you were a retailer, you might wrap your customers' purchases in eye-catching boxes, you might have a friendly assistant load the purchases into the customers' autos, and you might even deliver out-of-stock purchases directly to the customers' homes.

Every company has some collection of operational activities—things they do to deliver their products and services to their customers. You just want to be sure that your activities are part of an effective process, a structured and purposeful series of activities best designed to implement your strategies.

Remember that check-out lady at the specialty store in the Pike Place Market? She was implementing an operation (obtaining payment from the customer) necessary to the business's success (they need to collect revenues). But the check-out activity and her demeanor simply didn't fit with the store's high-end image and high prices.

Designing an operational process that accomplishes your strategies requires some careful thought. Oftentimes, it also requires that you change some operations that simply don't fit your business. The best way we know to accomplish this is to document your current activities, and then to improve those activities to fit your strategies.

You might choose to document your current activities by simply describing them in words. Alternatively, and the option we prefer, you might depict those activities in a diagram.

Using a diagram to illustrate your day-to-day operations allows you to see the overall pattern of activities at a glance. It also shows the interactions, and interdependencies, of the individuals and the groups within your organization. This makes it relatively easy to determine possible improvements for the overall process.

For example, the following diagram shows just a portion of the operational diagram for Mike's company. Mike runs a firm that does high-end residential remodeling; they turn good homes into spectacular living spaces. The diagram represents a small portion of the activities that Mike's company conducted before they made improvements in the process.

Operational Diagram Before Improvements

In this section of the operational diagram, Mike and his team described the steps that occurred when the internal walls of the new addition were put in place. In the early days of Mike's company, he thought that a quick sweep of the floor at day's end, and a time to retrieve all the nails dropped by his carpenters, were good ways to save costs.

After some experience and several interactions with customers, Mike realized two important things. First, he realized that he had been pursuing a false strategy to save costs. He determined that picking up nails at the end of the day (or at any time) was a money-losing activity. So, he deleted that step from his operations. His thought now was **Don't Pick Up Nails**.

Second, he found that his customers were very concerned about dust drifting into their current living space. So, Mike changed his operations to reflect these two new ideas. Here is the same portion of his operation with the new changes. You'll notice that the laborers now have time to help the carpenters with the roof, because they no longer are picking up nails.

Operational Diagram After Improvements

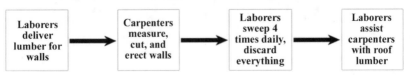

It turned out that Mike's customers were so concerned about dust in their homes that they wouldn't proceed with the project unless they were reassured that this wouldn't be an issue. Consequently, Mike's firm adopted two new activities to further prevent dust from entering the current living areas of the home. At the beginning of a project, not shown on the small section of the previous diagram, Mike's firm installs temporary partitions to segregate the work areas from the living spaces. And all throughout the project, the workers wear cloth shoe covers whenever they enter the customer's living spaces. This is all in keeping with the firm's strategy to provide distinguishing customer service.

Although Mike's firm is focused clearly on customer service, it can't ignore the operational efficiencies that will help it to make a profit. Thus, it has adopted the phrase *"Don't Pick Up Nails"* to represent the overall operating philosophy of the business: focus on the important things and ignore the many trivial activities that will only be distractions.

In contrast, let's assume that we created an operational process for a builder of tract homes. Their job is to build new homes in an efficient manner. These new homes are, of course, unoccupied.

In this case, the process would look somewhat different than Mike's. For instance, the tract home builder would not even consider daily sweepings, because there would be no homeowners to be concerned about the dust. Daily sweeping would present an unnecessary cost to the contractor and a distraction to the workers.

Furthermore, the tract home builder wouldn't adopt any of Mike's new activities. This firm certainly wouldn't install temporary dust barriers, nor would it have its workers wear booties.

We can see, then, that the creation of the firm's operational process clearly is driven by the customer. Whether your firm is a low-cost provider or a company that is differentiated by its products or its customer service, the operations of your firm should be focused on how to achieve the strategies that best serves your customers.

A Client's Story

One of our clients was a design/build company (they designed and then constructed beautiful public spaces in commercial buildings). Their work was stunning, and they completed their jobs in unusually short periods of time.

Sometimes, however, their profitability was below expectations. Intuitively, they knew that they must have some inefficiencies in their processes, but they couldn't pinpoint them.

They gathered the entire operational team for a nearly two-day session to map out their operational processes. They used large index cards to identify each step in the process, and taped the cards to the wall, with arrows showing the progression of the steps. There were some loops and diversions in the overall flow, but everything was documented.

Interestingly, there sometimes was disagreement about both the steps and their order. It was obvious that, through time, individuals had found a way to accomplish their role in a more desirable way. Unfortunately, they might not have informed others of their actions.

Even the operations manager of the company sat in wonder throughout this process as his team explained how things were actually getting done. He simply was unaware of some of the activities being undertaken, as were other members of the team when they learned about activities outside their own sphere of influence.

In the improvement step of the process, the team rearranged, added, and deleted index cards to produce a process that would best serve their customers, while also allowing them to operate more efficiently. When they were done, they had created a process that better served their customers, increased profitability, and provided them all with a common basis of understanding and future improvements.

A major benefit to documenting the process, whether by diagram or otherwise, is the transparency it provides to everyone in the firm. Engaging the entire team in the process is essential, because much of the operational knowledge, as well as many of the operational improvements, come from those directly involved in the operation, rather than exclusively from management. This also provides a common ground of shared creation; when everyone contributes, everyone takes pride in the end product. Over time, your firm should look continuously for ways to improve its operations. This will serve your customers in some better way and improve your firm as well.

CONSTANTLY BUILD THE CULTURE

We've described four of the five building blocks that allow you to build your operation around your client: define a good customer, create the right strategies for that good customer, create a sales process to secure and serve your good customer, and create an operations process to serve your good customer. The fifth building block is to constantly build a culture that embraces these first four building blocks.

Quite simply, your firm needs to incorporate these operational steps as part of its day-to-day activities. It will be a part of the company culture that everyone will value these activities and view them as essential to the success of the firm and its customers.

There are at least three steps that you can take to ensure that these activities become a part of your firm's culture. These are:

- Invest them with importance.
- Drive them home every day.
- Look for people who buy in.

Invest Them With Importance

In order to invest these activities with importance, you and the top management of your organization need to demonstrate through your actions that these activities are of high value. If the activities are really important, they will be a part of the day-to-day running of the company; you and the other managers will move from talking about them to using them as a regular tool for improvement.

Drive Them Home Every Day

The frequency of these focused activities also must be high. These are not once-a-year events, but rather daily activities that directly affect the performance of your firm. Thus, every strategic discussion in your firm should include some aspect of these building blocks.

For example, if the company decided to take on a new target market, it likely would need to adopt a new sales process and a new operational process to serve that market. So, you'd bring the team together to create those new processes, thus involving the team in an important activity and responding in the best way to a significant change to the business.

Look for People Who Buy In

Finally, your company should actively enlist people who embrace these activities. Changing the company's culture, even in small ways, is usually a difficult undertaking. People who are enthusiastic about the company's changes are enormously valuable in the overall process, and the company should coach and encourage them to be motivating leaders and coaches for the rest of the team.

Points to Remember

- Use the five building blocks to design your company around your customer.
  - Define the right customers.
  - Create the right strategies for that good customer.
  - Create a sales process to secure and serve your good customers.
  - Create an operations process to serve your good customers.
  - Constantly build the culture.
- Embrace one of the three generic strategies.
  - Low cost.
  - Differentiated products.
  - Differentiated customer service.
- Create detailed and specific strategies for your business.
- Use best-practice processes to ensure that you'll achieve your goals.
  - Sales process.
  - Operational processes.
- Use repetition, frequency, and key employees to constantly build the culture.

CHAPTER 5

Empower your entire team

A Client's Story

One of our clients was a wholesale supplier to retail stores. The CEO of the company was always very busy—harried and overwhelmed by the demands of clients as well as staff.

We discovered fairly quickly that virtually all the staff reported to the CEO, either formally or informally. If they needed something, they simply made a visit to the CEO's office and got the attention they wanted.

One day, during a conversation we were having with the CEO, one of the staff members politely interrupted us. She wanted approval for some display materials to be used at an upcoming trade show.

We looked on in amazement as the CEO chose from a variety of relatively low-cost products to assemble a group of display items that would be used at the trade show. The staff member smiled in satisfaction and left to assemble the items on a display board.

We learned later that this was typical behavior for both the staff and this top manager. The most minute details needed the CEO's approval, and the staff members were well trained to seek this approval at every turn.

So here was an example of a manager who was involved in every detail of the business. No one did anything of substance, or made any decisions, without this CEO's approval. And, of course, the business couldn't operate without this person's presence. Vacations and indeed absences of any kind were out of the question for this manager, who was compelled to be present at all times to run the show.

———————————— A Client's Story ————————————

Another of our clients was a company that provided high-level communications expertise to its client companies. These clients were highly demanding, and each one had a set of virtually unique requirements and desires for the equipment and techniques it used for its internal and external communications.

The CEO of this company was well aware of the importance of keeping his clients happy, and he spent long hours as a hands-on manager to ensure that his company performed at a high level. But he yearned for something more.

This CEO wanted to be less involved! He wanted to be able to take a two-week vacation and not be compelled to call his office multiple times a day—or even once a day. He wanted his company to run well when he wasn't there.

And this is exactly what happened. Over time this CEO learned how to create a company that adhered to his vision and principles but did not require his constant presence. He took several multi-week vacations without calling his office, and the company did better than ever.

———————————————————————————————

There is quite a contrast between these two CEOs, isn't there? One is a micro-manager, reveling in the importance of making numerous day-to-day decisions, while training the staff to seek constant approval. The other is a manager who learned how to empower his team to accomplish his vision, without his constant presence. This frees him from the day-to-day demands and allows him to work on his business rather than in his business—or to take a vacation.

HOW CAN YOU EMPOWER YOUR TEAM?

Many of us have observed that, as an entrepreneurial organization grows, it often encounters difficulties that are termed to be "people problems," "organizational plateaus," or "that difficult size between a small company and a big company." This also occurs commonly in departments within larger firms.

When we look closely, however, we see that these difficulties arise from a crisis in management. This is shown in the following diagram, the Life Cycle of a Manager, and then explained by our friend Mike, during a presentation about his company to a local business organization.

The Life Cycle of a Manager

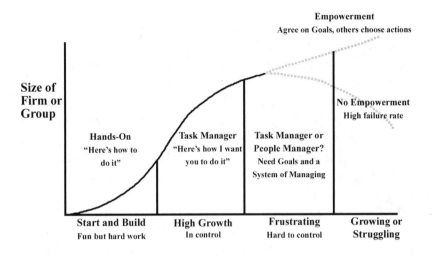

Mike's Company

"**H**ere's the deal," says Mike. "When we start a business, or when we start a new department in a company, everything is very hands on. We are involved in everything, and we do all the things that need to be done.

"This is lots of fun if you're an entrepreneurial type person. At this stage, you figure out what works and what doesn't. And after you figure out what works, you're pretty convinced that you know what you're doing. After all, it works.

"Now, in the second stage of development, you do less yourself because you have other people to do things. But you're still close enough to the ground to know what needs to be done, and how to do it. After all, you invented the ways to do it. So you instruct your folks to do things a certain way—the way that you already determined worked for you.

"This second stage is often a time of high growth, and it can be very exciting. You see your company or your department grow and prosper, and you find yourself with a great increase in power and influence. Now you've got a real crew of people working for you, and they're helping to carry out your instructions and your vision. And they're very excited about the high growth and the opportunities for them.

"The third stage is where things get dicey. Now you have too many people to watch closely every day. The hands-on management method (I'll do it myself) and the task management method (I'll show you exactly how I did it) that worked so well in the early stages of growth become, ironically, a serious liability. You're simply not able to do everything yourself or even watch everyone else closely enough to ensure that they'll do it exactly as you would.

"The symptoms of this situation manifest themselves with both managers and employees. Managers can't understand why 'I have to do it myself if I want it done right,' and employees can't understand why they're 'being micro-managed at some times and being expected to guess what my manager wants at other times.'

"This can become a highly frustrating time for everyone. The demands of the growing business are relentless, and managers now find themselves in 'crisis management mode." The longer this situation persists, the greater is the risk of company failure.

"But that, of course, depends upon what is done to launch the fourth phase. This is where managers really have two major choices. They can continue to try to manage things as they did in the early stages, or they can create a system that will allow employees to choose their own paths toward meeting their goals."

MANAGEMENT WOULD BE EASY IF YOU DIDN'T HAVE TO DEAL WITH PEOPLE

To succeed in this fourth phase requires the manager to transition from a do-it-my-way approach to the "people management business." For the majority of managers, this is a difficult assignment, especially if they started out on their own or with a very small group.

People management does not come easy to these managers. They like the day to day activities as long as they can do them on their own. The very idea of spending lots of time "hand holding" others may be very uncomfortable and quite different from the managers' original vision, which held only them, and their ideas, at its focal point. Many times, of course, these folks simply haven't been trained to be a manager, so it's another unknown, and most folks already have enough unknowns.

We frequently remind managers, as well as aspiring managers, that management is a new career. As surely as teaching is different from accounting, management is different from the role that a person held as an employee or as a start-up entrepreneur.

Mike's Company

" I n the past, right here in our company, we immediately took our best carpenter and made him the lead carpenter. We don't do that anymore. Now, we make sure that we have a lead carpenter who has the talents and skills to manage a crew properly, before we make him a manager.

"The natural ability part of this is especially important to us. We want to be sure that all our managers have the natural ability and inclination to coach and motivate their people. We don't try to teach these things to people that don't exhibit a natural inclination; we look for people who already have these abilities. We do, however, spend significant effort to train and coach our managers to acquire new skills and knowledge that will make them more effective.

"In addition, we also focus strongly on the management process itself. The idea here is to provide as much training and support as we can. We know that we need clarity, communication, and commitment. This is critical to the success of the manager and of our company."

ENABLING REAL EMPOWERMENT

An empowered environment allows you take full advantage of the capabilities of your team. The notion is not for you to conceive, plan, and do everything yourself but rather for you to encourage and coach others to achieve as much as they can. This allows you to do other things such as work *on* your business rather than *in* it.

We know that management isn't an easy job, and we know that it's really an entirely new career. So how can you empower your team so that you can be a highly successful manager? We believe that the answer to this question has at least three parts, all of which are designed to produce a condition of real empowerment.

First, you should create clear and powerful goals for everyone on your team. You also should have a keen interest in the achievement of these goals, and less interest in the precise ways by which those goals are accomplished (with some caveats, which we'll explain).

Second, you must provide clear and consistent guidance to everyone on the team regarding the rules by which they must operate. Just as we all must obey the rules of the road when we drive, so too must your team members adhere to your guidelines and principles.

Third, you must be convinced that your team members meet some very specific conditions related to their competency, principles, and reliability. When they do, you can allow them to achieve their goals in their own way, as long as they stay within the boundaries.

GOALS AND BOUNDARIES

We're going to use some diagrams to show you how this all works. In all of the diagrams, we use a target as a symbol for the goals of the position and an "X" as a symbol for the starting place of the person in that position.

Manager's route to a goal

The first diagram, labeled Manager's Route to a Goal, illustrates the path that you, as the manager, would take to achieve the goal. Perhaps you started the business or the department, or perhaps you already held the position responsible for this goal. Nevertheless, you've already acquired the skills and experience to achieve this goal, and you know exactly how to do it. To you, it's a straight line: You do some activities in a certain way, and there you are at the goal. Simple.

Manager's Route to a Goal

Goal

X
Start Here

Establishing the boundaries

Your knowledge of how to achieve the goal becomes especially important as you move from being hands-on to being a task manager, as you move from phase one to phase two in the diagram we showed you before, the Life Cycle of a Manager. As you begin to have other people around to help you, you perhaps couldn't be more certain that you know how to get things done. After all, you invented the method, and all these other folks are new. So, you'll likely be inclined to instruct others to do things as you did ("do it my way").

─────────────── **Mike's Company** ───────────────

"Once a manager acquires a few employees, she can't possibly watch them all closely enough to ensure that they do everything the way that she would. Besides, she shouldn't be watching employees that closely anyway. She should be planning her business, determining what her customers want, and coaching her team to achieve the goals.

"So, we give the employees as much responsibility and authority as they can assume to reach their goals. The less intervention required by us, the more time we have for other things.

"But we can't merely set them loose. That would be chaos. We need to help them understand their boundaries.

"Let me give you an analogy. Suppose that we decided to send someone on a road trip to a specific city and told them that all they had to do was get to that city.

"We might find that they arrived in a timely manner without incident. We might also find, however, that they got there much later than we hoped or that they got four speeding tickets on the way. Without any guidance, or boundaries, anything might be possible.

"In our diagram here, titled Enabling Empowerment: Establishing the Boundaries, the employee has a goal, but we're not allowing him to do absolutely anything to reach it. We're asking him to work within defined boundaries, ground rules, and principles. And some of these boundaries are obvious. For example, we don't want them to do anything illegal or unethical.

Enabling Empowerment: Establishing the Boundaries

Boundaries	Boundaries
Rules	Rules
Principles	Principles
Legal	Legal
Ethical	Ethical
Mission	Mission
Vision	Vision
Clear Goals	Clear Goals
On Time	On Time
Strategies	Strategies
Position	Position
Description	Description
Reward	Reward
Program	Program
System of	System of
Managing	Managing

X
Start Here

"You'll notice that one of the items on the list is the position description. This is the detailed description of the goals and responsibilities of the position that we discussed previously. All of the other items are common to everyone in the company.

"So, let's be clear about what this diagram tells our employees. It says that they can achieve their goals however they see fit, as long as they stay within bounds. You'll notice also that "time" is one of the boundaries; the goals must be achieved within a certain time period.

"These ideas can be challenging to a manager, especially a manager who is new to this system. I know that they were a big challenge for me when I first started using this system.

"It drove me nuts to watch people take a path that was not the one I knew was right. Sure, I wanted them to make their goals, and I told myself that I'd let them do it in their own way.

"Most of the time, I just left them alone at first, assuming that they'd know what to do in their jobs. At some point, though, I'd discover that some folks weren't doing things the way I expected. So, I'd jump in with both feet to correct them. And I did this even when they were clearly in bounds. I just didn't like the way they did things.

"But they didn't really want my help. They accused me of micromanagement, and they clearly didn't want that. Anyway, through time, and with some coaching that I got from business colleagues and my employees, I finally learned to let go. After all, the goal is the goal, the goal is not to do it my way."

Early steps to goal achievement

In the next diagram, titled Enabling Empowerment: Early Steps to Goal Achievement, we witness the early progress of the employee in attempting to achieve his goals. Although he's still in bounds, he's zig-zagging all over the place. He's simply not doing things the way the manager would do them. This is what drives many managers crazy. Why is he doing all that zig-zagging?

Enabling Empowerment: Early Steps to Goal Achievement

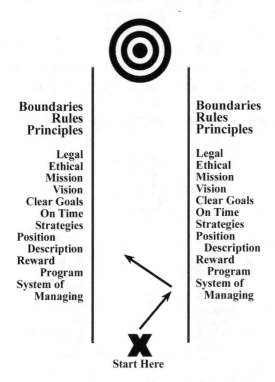

It is helpful, however, to remind yourself that the path to the goal is straight only because you defined it that way. You concluded that your way was the correct way. But is it the only correct way?

You can begin to free yourself of the management-crisis dilemma when you appreciate two basic facts. First, you can become a highly successful manager only when you can empower others to carry out your vision. Second, the means that others use to reach the goals may be different from yours, while still being effective.

Thus, you can enable others to reach the goals by allowing them to choose their own means of getting there. So, do you get what you want? Yes, if what you want is attaining the goals. No, if what you want is strict conformity to your means of getting there.

Out of Bounds

Now let's look at what happens when the employee doesn't stay within bounds. In this case, the employee has crossed the boundaries. Perhaps he is behind schedule. Or perhaps he has violated the guidelines for dealing with customers. For whatever reason, he's out of bounds.

Enabling Empowerment: Corrective Action Needed

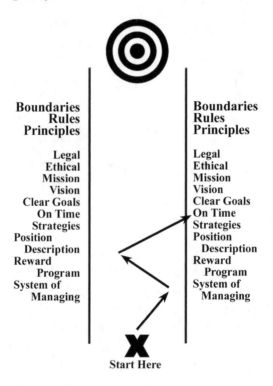

--------------- Mike's Company ---------------

"Now we have a situation," says Mike, "where the employee has crossed the boundaries. "So what happens? This is where our manager gets involved in establishing some corrective action and some coaching. The company simply won't allow this.

"If it happens infrequently, as is usually the case, we expect our coaching to produce improved performance. If it happens more than we expect, we may need to find that employee a new position, and perhaps that position is with another company. But the behavior won't be allowed to continue.

"You'll notice that the employee came very close to the boundary earlier on in the process. Perhaps it appeared that he would miss a deadline. At this point, or even beforehand, the supervisor may have coached him to get him back on track—or perhaps he figured it out on his own. Since he got back on track, it appears that something worked.

"One of the valuable things about this system is that the goals and boundaries are clear. So, we know when we're on track, we know when we're out of bounds, and we know when corrective action is needed."

Reaching the Goal

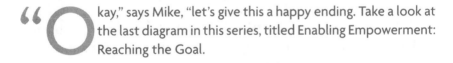

Mike's Company

"Okay," says Mike, "let's give this a happy ending. Take a look at the last diagram in this series, titled Enabling Empowerment: Reaching the Goal.

Enabling Empowerment: Reaching the Goal

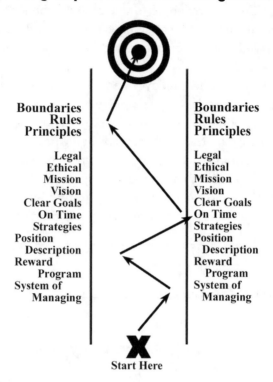

"The employee has now reached his goal. He has stayed within bounds, perhaps with a bit of extra coaching when he got very close to the boundary. But he achieved his goal, and he achieved it on time. Don't forget that achieving the goal within a certain time is one of the boundaries.

"Although he didn't take the straight line I might have taken, he accomplished his goal on time. He was, therefore, successful. He didn't do it my way, but he succeeded. And perhaps it turned out that his way was even more effective than mine—much as I might not like to admit it sometimes," Mike says with a good natured smile.

CONDITIONS FOR EMPOWERMENT

We realize that so far this empowerment process looks fairly easy. Set the goals for everyone, establish their boundaries, and set 'em all loose.

As you might guess, it isn't quite that simple. But it's not too far off really.

Before a manager can put a team member in an empowered environment, the manager must be satisfied that the team member can meet some very specific conditions. They're quite straightforward, but they are absolutely critical.

Mike's Company

"Think about this for a moment," says Mike. "We've employed a system that liberates managers from constant oversight, while allowing employees the responsibility and accountability to achieve goals as they see fit.

"Let's look a bit more closely at what's required in order for employees to assume this kind of accountability and responsibility. This is not a system of anarchy or neglect. We purposely put the employees on a path to achieve clear goals, but we do it in a way that frees up the manager from close and constant oversight.

"There are three steps that we follow to ensure that our employees are correctly empowered, that they have both the responsibility and authority to conduct their activities effectively. We've already talked a bit about the first two.

"The first step is to establish the goals for every employee. As we discussed earlier, goals should be unambiguous, measurable, challenging, and yet reasonable. In fact, our managers work closely with everyone on their teams to establish and agree upon each person's goals.

"The second step is to establish some rules, or boundaries. As we've already seen, we need to be clear with everyone about the rules of the road, and there are certain boundaries that they simply shouldn't cross.

"The third step is to ensure that the correct conditions exist between the manager and the employee, in order to allow the employee to be empowered to reach the goals in her own way. This third step is critical, but oftentimes it isn't even considered. We've found that without these conditions, the employee and the manager are doomed to failure. There are three of these conditions, all of which are equally important, and all of which must be demonstrated by the employee to the manager:

1. Shared principles.
2. Reliability.
3. Competency.

The following diagram illustrates these three conditions. In order for anyone to be empowered effectively, they must share the principles of the manager and the organization, be reliable, and be competent.

Conditions for Empowerment

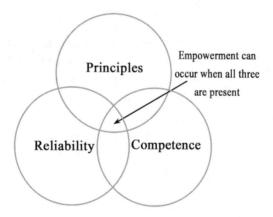

All three of these conditions are necessary, and this is depicted by the rounded triangular area in the middle of the diagram. Two out of three isn't enough. The person in the position must exhibit all three conditions in order for a manager to empower her to achieve her goals on time and within bounds.

In effect, these three conditions are a type of boundary, but they deserve special attention because they often describe fundamental impediments for even initiating true empowerment. Managers sometimes overlook the need for these three conditions, probably because they are of a non-quantitative, or "soft," nature. They are, admittedly, very easy to ignore.

Mike's Company

"The circle labeled 'Principles,'" says Mike, "represents those moral, ethical, and other issues that must be shared, and agreed to, between supervisor and employee. These are standard rules of personal conduct that reflect the underlying beliefs of our company. Only when our principles are shared by our employees should we be willing to empower them to conduct activities on our behalf."

"You know, Mike," says a lady in the back, "this hits close to home. I had an employee that really knew his stuff, and he was as reliable as the day is long when it came to delivering on time, but I knew that he was not an honest guy. I just couldn't allow myself to put him in a highly responsible position."

"So, what did you do?" asks a fellow up front.

"Well, one day he really crossed the line. I had to fire him."

"One of the toughest things I discovered," says Mike, "is that I shouldn't try to save people from their own principles. I used to work hard with folks like the guy you described, thinking that I could turn them around. After all, they've got all these other good qualities. What I found, though, was that I was wasting my time—time that I could have spent with the top performers in my company. And the top performers are the ones who will make my company great."

Lots of heads are nodding. "Does that mean that you should just let these people go?" asks another fellow.

"Well, here's an answer that you might not like to hear, but yes. When you know that an employee does not share your principles, it's time for a divorce.

"There are, of course, civilized means of parting ways. But, as an example, I haven't yet found a method to turn a dishonest person into an honest one. And even if I knew how, it would take too much time away from the interactions I should be having with my top performers."

"You know, Mike," says the lady in the back, "you keep referring to the time spent with your top performers. I thought that the idea was to leave the top performers alone, because they already know what to do, and to spend time teaching the weaker performers how to improve."

"Yeah," says Mike, "that's what I thought, too. But then one of my friends pointed out that the company does much better when I spend time with my top performers. These are the folks that already are motivated, focused, and goal-oriented. They already have a great attitude, which is critical to us, and so I just have to coach them about the easy things. You know, things like the little bits of knowledge that they may be missing to turn that mediocre project into a great one."

You'll have your own list of principles, but as an example here are some principles that have been relevant to our clients. Bear in mind that principles are inviolate (they don't change with the season or by whim). They are reliable and unchanging cornerstones of the company culture and the values represented by the company.

EXAMPLE PRINCIPLES

- **Legal and ethical issues.**
- **Company vision and mission.**
- **Company goals and strategies.**
- **Management system.**
- **Position descriptions.**

Some of these items may not seem to fit a traditional definition of a principle. For example, though you may think of certain ethical issues as principles, you may not think of the company vision, goals, or position description as principles.

As Mike pointed out, however, principles are standard rules of personal conduct that reflect the underlying beliefs of your organization. You need everyone to agree to the vision, goals, and position descriptions; otherwise, you'll have an organization that is fractured and inefficient at best. Like a team of sled dogs, everyone has to be pulling in the same direction.

A Client's Story

O ne of our client companies was founded by two highly-creative and technically skilled individuals. Through the years, the company grew steadily and had become highly respected by both clients and employees. The owners were quite proud of what they'd built, and rightly so.

Along the way, as the company grew larger, the owners decided to hire an individual who would take a top management role and also might become an owner as well. The owners were not enthusiastic sales or marketing people, and the new individual was just that: a passionate marketer and salesman. Conversely, whereas the owners were creative and highly technical, the new individual lacked these skills.

The owners believed that the new individual had skills that were complementary to theirs, and that together they could be a strong team. The new guy and his team would bring in the work, and the owners and their teams would get the work done. The company would grow, the new guy would become a partner, and the future would be bright.

As time progressed, however, so too did the complexities of the relationships between the owners and the new guy. The underlying question was whether these were differences of style or substance.

Quite simply, the owners had done things their way for quite some time, and now this new guy was upsetting the apple cart. Where the owners had relied on a collegial and harmonious culture at the headquarters, the new fellow was implementing strong aggressive tactics to acquire new clients, putting unusual and strong demands on the staff to support him. Additionally, he tended to operate in a more autonomous and autocratic fashion, rather than take the more traditional collegial tack.

This new approach often required short internal deadlines to produce the desired marketing and sales materials needed to impress a new client. Additionally, the new fellow's manner could sometimes be abrupt, impolite, and even rude. His viewpoint was that he got the job done, he captured new clients effectively, and people were just too sensitive.

As time progressed further, the owners became increasingly upset by the way that the new guy treated the other employees. Whereas he might have previously acted impatient or sometimes rude, he now exhibited distain for other employees. He thought that they just "didn't get it" and that his way was the right way. He continued to operate this way despite widespread feedback that he was alienating the other employees, who should be his allies.

This began to carry over in the relationship between the new guy and the owners as well. There grew, over time, a wide gap in philosophy and approach to both clients and employees.

In the end, the owners parted ways with this new guy. In short, they did not share principles, which in this case amounted to standards of behavior. The way that the owners treated fellow employees, and each other, was fundamentally different from the way that the new sales guy treated everyone.

Interestingly, after this individual left the company, the culture rebounded to "normal," staff morale rose, and, not surprisingly, business was better than ever. Why should that be the case? When everyone started to work together again, rather than bicker and push back, the effectiveness of the sales and marketing efforts actually improved. After all, there was a team of people doing things together now, not just one "star."

Mike's Company

"Think about the circle labeled 'Reliability,' Mike says. "I'm reminded of a friend who drove to visit me at my new home. I asked him if he found my directions satisfactory, and he replied: 'I made a right turn exactly four miles after the interstate highway exit, just like you told me. Not surprisingly, there was a road there, exactly when I made the turn.' He's a great friend, but you get the idea. Your word must be good, time after time. You must do what you say, always, so that people can rely upon you.

"Building reliability reminds us of building a nice house. It takes real work to create it, but when you do, it has long-lasting value. As a practical matter, reliability often can be built through day-to-day interactions, and that is how we foster it here. We put people together in situations that require them to rely upon one another for the project to be successful."

"Mike," asks a fellow in the back row, "this one is a problem for me. I've got a fellow working at my company that everyone loves. He's just a great guy, and he works very hard. And he tries to help everyone he can. The problem is that he often is late on his work and on his promises. But I really can't ask him to work any harder."

"Mike," interjects a lady in the third row, "do you mind if I answer this? I had a situation just like this in my company."

"Please go ahead," Mike says.

"Well," says the lady, "we realized after months of this behavior that we were at fault, not the employee. Oh sure, he was not meeting his deadlines, but we weren't coaching him properly on setting expectations with his co-workers. He needed to really understand his own capabilities and the importance of meeting his commitments, and we needed to coach him on this. After a while, he learned when to say no, and he focused on meeting his existing commitments rather than trying to please everyone."

"That's a great success story," says Mike. "Actually, we've found that the type of employee you've described is one of the hardest to manage. First, he creates a high level of good will with his personality and his willingness to help others. Then he leaves us disappointed, and sometimes in real trouble, when he doesn't deliver. But his positive attitude continues to convince us that we've got a great employee on board. And he is a great employee, but only when we've coached him successfully as you described."

For true empowerment to work in your organization, everyone on the team must be reliable. For those who aren't, we believe that about half are coachable. That is, like the lady in Mike's example, you'll be able to turn an unreliable team member into a reliable one about half the time.

This is still a risky proposition for you as a manager, because half your time on these activities will be squandered. But it is considerably more optimistic that attempting to coach principles, which we believe to be a virtually useless exercise.

There are a couple things you can do to increase your probabilities of success here, and they are related to the personalities of your unreliable folks. Our experience is that these unreliable folks are often of two types: those who have a great attitude but don't deliver, and those who don't possess a very positive attitude.

You can guess where we're going with this. We think your time is best spent with the folks who have a good attitude; you have a reasonable chance of coaching them to budget their time, set proper expectations, and understand their own limits. The folks with the wrong attitude may, in many cases, find success in another organization. Remember: Everyone can be successful in the right environment. It just might not be your environment.

———— A Client's Story ————

One of our client companies was owned by several individuals with complementary technical, administrative, and sales talents. On paper, they appeared to be a good team, with combined abilities that covered most of the essential functions of the business. In fact, if you just read their resumes, you'd likely conclude that this was a winning team.

Over time, however, the behavior of one of these individuals became increasingly problematic. And it had nothing to do with anything that might be on a resume.

More specifically, this owner was not reliable. When meetings were scheduled for 9:00 a.m., he'd walk in at 9:15, or later. When a deadline was established, he'd miss it.

Invariably, there was some excuse such as traffic, needed to take Susie to school, a customer called, and so forth. His partners were highly frustrated, but they were not assertive enough to bring the issue to a discussion.

In our early engagement with the owners, we stated that we expected them to start their meetings on time. To do otherwise was to be disrespectful of others' time and commitment. They all agreed, and they all complied with meeting times and deadlines.

Over time, however, as it became increasingly clear that his partners would not hold him accountable, the wayward owner reverted back to form. Once again, he consistently arrived late to meetings, and he regularly missed his deadlines.

As a result, his partners merely repeated their discussions upon his late arrivals at meetings. They became increasingly frustrated, but still wouldn't discuss the issue with him.

Finally, after the frustration had sufficient time to sour the relationships and create a highly emotional state among the owners, they decided to dissolve their partnership. Even that didn't look good on paper.

Mike's Company

"The last circle," says Mike, "represents 'Competency.' This, of course, is critical to effective performance and to our willingness to empower someone. None of us would purposely put incompetent people in any position, especially positions of high influence.

"In our company, we put a great deal of thought and effort into our interview process in order to assess the competency of our prospective employees. We look for several things.

"First, we want them to have a minimum set of skills and knowledge to do the job. But we're not necessarily looking for the person with the strongest set of skills.

"And that's because what we really look for is a person who has naturally occurring characteristics that will allow him to excel at the position. These are most important to us.

"For example, when we look for a new manager, we look for someone who loves to coach and who has a natural ability to work with others on an individual basis. They treat each person as someone special, because they are, and they love to coach that person to bring out their best.

"Similarly, when we look for someone to work in our accounting department, we look for someone who loves numbers. This is the person who will stay up all night to get the numbers to agree to the last penny. But this is something they love, and they're very good at it."

One of the ladies in the audience starts laughing. Everyone turns to see what the joke is.

"Sorry," she says, "I'm just now aware that I couldn't get a job in your accounting department. I let the bank tell me how much money I have in my checking account!"

"That's okay," says Mike. "You no doubt have other naturally occurring characteristics that would allow you to excel at some other position. One of our important jobs as managers is to fit you to the correct position."

"Yeah," says another lady, "this makes a lot of sense. We should try to find people that have naturally occurring characteristics that fit the requirements of the position. I'm thinking of your managers, the ones who love to coach and to treat each person as someone with individual needs. Since they love to do this, they probably do it consistently well. I know that's the case with me. I love to eat chocolate, and I do it very well."

"You've hit on an important point," says Mike while still smiling broadly. "When we put people in a position that allows them to use their naturally occurring characteristics, we get naturally occurring high-level performance.

"This is in contrast, of course, with choosing folks who seem to have the right experience but lack the right attitude or lack some other naturally occurring characteristic needed. With these folks, we bring them on board as a top-quality hire and then later fire them as an incompetent."

"So," asks the lady again, "you're saying that it's our fault for hiring them in the first place?"

"It many cases it is, although sometimes the candidate can fool us. But we hired them for a position in which they were unable to perform. Sure, they had some experience, but they didn't have the natural characteristics needed. So, they didn't perform well. They had to force themselves every day to compute that table of numbers, or someone else had to remind them. In the long run, it doesn't work.

"The search for competent employees is a difficult one, and this topic could keep us busy for the rest of the night. But I urge you to focus on this activity, because there is little else of more importance to your firm than filling it with outstanding people."

Finding and coaching competent team members is, of course, a key responsibility of a highly successful manager. But how much teaching, coaching, and training can a manager do to help bring a person to a competent level?

We believe that there are three components to competency: knowledge, experience, and natural ability. Although knowledge can be taught, and experience can be gained over time, natural ability is not coachable.

We can hear some of you saying, "Come on. I coached someone in a new area and they turned out to love the work and they did an outstanding job." We believe you; you may in fact have done just that.

But we also believe that there were probably 99 other incidents where it didn't work—coaching someone lacking in the right natural ability did not produce a high performer. And we don't think it's worth your time and effort to embark on an activity with such a very low success rate. You should be spending that time with your high performers.

A Client's Story

One of our clients was a highly technical consulting company that provided its customers with expertise in the design and oversight of their communications systems. They were real champs in their marketplace, and they were sought by virtually all of the blue ribbon companies in their city.

Most of the work done by the company was generated by word of mouth or by additional projects generated by current or past customers. This is fairly common in well-regarded service firms, who often do not rely upon new customers for a significant portion of their revenues.

On the other hand, in order to grow aggressively, the company did have a senior level salesperson whose responsibility was to generate work from new customers. As these customers came on board, the company was confident that it could turn them into steady customers who also would return regularly for additional services.

After more than a year of service with the company, the salesperson had not generated any significant new work. In discussions with this person, it was fairly obvious that she lacked competency for this position.

For example, when it was decided that companies in a certain market should be contacted, the sales person wanted to collect ever-more-perfect information before making the contact. And when meeting about strategies, she would lean back in her chair and settle in for long discussions, which she would initiate and sustain.

This salesperson was not, of course, all bad. She was reliable. She did what she said she'd do (she just wouldn't commit to doing what was really needed). She also shared the same principles as the other managers and owners.

What she lacked was competency. She simply did not have the acquired skills or the natural abilities to be a great salesperson.

The company parted ways with this person and put another individual in the sales position. The new person had the competency and natural abilities to excel, and indeed he did. The company achieved record sales.

WIDE BOULEVARDS, HIGH CURBS

You can see that when you have the right people, who you can fully empower, you can give them increasing responsibilities and goals. As a result, they can accomplish great things.

We think of this as "wide boulevards, high curbs." The team has lots of latitude, but the goals and the boundaries are clear and unambiguous.

THE PROCESS AS A DIAGNOSTIC TOOL

Establishing the framework for empowerment is a key step for your organization, and the empowerment process we've described here is designed to guide everyone in your organization in achieving their goals. It establishes the goals, sets boundaries, and provides criteria for the conditions that must exist for empowerment to occur.

The empowerment process also is a very effective means for diagnosing why goals are not being met. In this case, you can look at the boundaries, to ensure that they have been properly set and explained, and you also can look at the three-circle diagram to determine if there is some lack of principles, reliability, or competence.

As an illustration, let's assume that the proper goals have been established, that the boundaries have been set and explained correctly, but that the goals are not being met. You can then turn to the three-circle diagram to look for an explanation corresponding to one of the three circles.

For example, it might be that the employee is violating principles. Perhaps he is operating in a way that is contrary to your vision, or is offending customers, or is violating company policies. This requires corrective action on your part, in order to get the employee back on the path to meeting the goals or to place the employee in a more appropriate position (whether in your company or elsewhere).

If the breach in principles is a misunderstanding on the part of the employee, or is something done in ignorance, you may decide that some coaching and training are quite sufficient. If, on the other hand, the breach in principles arises from a fundamental difference in viewpoints between the company and the employee (for example, has distain for customers or for the company vision), you likely will need to take strong action, perhaps leading to the employee's separation from your organization. As we mentioned previously, we don't believe it's worthwhile for you to try to instill new principles in your team members.

Alternatively, you might determine that the employee and the company share principles, but that the employee is unreliable or not sufficiently competent. In either event, you can diagnose the problem to determine if coaching and training can provide a solution (has the right attitude, skills, and experience) or if, instead, you must take more drastic measures (is lacking in needed natural abilities).

Points to Remember

- As a company or group grows in size, the manager is challenged to either assume increasing close-management responsibilities, which eventually becomes un-sustainable, or to create an environment of empowerment.

- Management is a new career, requiring different natural abilities than the previous position held. People management is critical.

- Highly successful managers:
  - Create clear goals.
  - Establish clear boundaries.
  - Empower their teams to achieve their goals when the members have:
    - Competency.
    - Shared principles.
    - Reliability.
  - Create wide boulevards and high curbs for their team.

- You can use the empowerment process as a diagnostic tool. You can diagnose why goals are not being met, whether the person in the position is capable of meeting the goals, and the likelihood that you can coach them effectively to meet the goals.

CHAPTER 6

Do the right things right

────────────────── A Fable ──────────────────

The airline captain checked his instruments again to be sure that he read them correctly. He could hardly believe it, but it was true: The plane was moving at a record speed. They must have a terrific tail wind, whisking them along at this kind of pace. What a feeling!

He now checked some other instruments as well. Although the news here was not as good, he still was buoyed by the news of his terrific speed.

He decided to share this news with his passengers. He picked up the intercom mike, took a slow breath, and spoke in his classic Chuck Yeager style.

"Ladies and Gentlemen," he said, "I want to tell you about our progress. I have both good and bad news. The good news is that we are making great time. Our ground speed is 70 knots above normal. The bad news, however, is that we're lost. I don't have a clue where we are."

──

Business owners frequently talk to themselves. If nothing else, it's a way to converse with like-minded people.

If only the day were 32 hours long, we say to ourselves. Then I could get all my stuff done.

We know, of course, that even if the day were 42 hours long, we'd still not have enough time. We always manage to line up more tasks than can be accomplished. Just like the airplane pilot, we're going at a record pace. But do we know if we're going in the right direction?

A SYSTEM OF MANAGING

The trick is not to create a 32 hour day but rather to focus on the activities that are the *Vital Few*—and to learn to ignore the *trivial many*. Thus, the solution to the dilemma is not to search for more hours, but to accomplish the things that are essential while ignoring the time-wasting activities.

The best way that we know to provide company-wide focus on the *vital few* is to employ a system of managing—a consistent set of procedures and principles that guide us to do the Right Things Right. This management system must focus everyone on their goals while allowing flexibility and choice on how the goals will be accomplished. It also provides a common language to everyone, compelling them to communicate in ways that are harmonious with the company's vision and goals. And it must compel everyone to avoid the *trivial many*.

We readily admit that there are many ways to manage a company, some of which are actually successful, and some of these successful ways are themselves widely divergent in their nature. They range from tightly controlled autocracies to seemingly unstructured organizations. For example, imagine how different the management system at Apple must be from Wal-Mart.

We'll describe here a proven and effective system of managing, a system that can be applied to virtually any company. This system provides at least three benefits by:

- Focusing everyone on goals all the time.
- Providing everyone with clear guidelines.
- Rewarding everyone when the company goals are achieved.

A Client's Story

Years ago, we met with a company in steep decline. It had once been quite successful, but it had not adapted to changes in its marketplace.

It was quickly obvious that this company was experiencing managerial chaos, and that the current managers did not know how to turn things around. Though many firms exhibit some of the behaviors we saw, this new client was in real trouble.

First, they had no means of tracking or managing their progress in attaining any goals. And the goals themselves were only vaguely defined (such as "make more sales").

Second, they had no mechanism for aligning the managers and staff to do "the right things right" every day. The managers all worked hard, and they wanted to achieve success, both for the company and themselves. But every week was a mystery on how to achieve success; they were in a perpetual cycle of get the work done, get more work, hope for a good outcome. They were in a hamster wheel.

Third, the overall quality of communications among the managers and staff was poor: It was infrequent, unfocused, and open-ended. Many times, people walked into a meeting wondering what it was about and then walked away wondering if anything had been accomplished. Some of the same topics seemed to be recycled time and again.

Fourth, the managers and staff didn't communicate well about the specifics of what needed to be done. The managers continually complained about employees who didn't do what they should, and the employees complained about lack of clarity and changes in direction.

Fifth, the managers were inconsistent about their accountability. Despite their titles and perceptions about their positions, they frequently had conflicts with each other about what they should accomplish. And these conflicts were often situational in nature: They surfaced when a problem emerged, and they were discussed in an emotionally-charged atmosphere.

Sixth, despite the great depth of experience and knowledge among the managers, they didn't often share their insights with others in a productive or non-confrontational way. Instead, they used their knowledge as an argumentative weapon rather than a tool for collective productivity.

As the old saying goes, "Other than that, Mrs. Lincoln, how did you like the play?" This was a company that needed a system of management.

The Three Cs of an Effective System of Managing

An effective system of managing combines three key attributes: clarity, communication, and commitment. Together, these three attributes focus the management team and the entire company on the important goals and actions that must be accomplished.

1. **Clarity**: The management system should provide an effective means of providing everyone with a clear and unambiguous view of the important actions to be taken—today and every day. It should focus everyone's attention on the goals to be accomplished and the strategies and actions required to attain those goals.

2. **Communication**: The management system should provide an inherently effective means of communication among all members of the company. We know that we can't keep everyone informed about all the issues, but we can use a system of managing that provides effective communication among the right people for the right issues.

3. **Commitment**: To be effective, the management system must engender strong commitment from everyone in the company. Such commitment is itself constructed from three key factors:

   - Responsibility: We want people to take ownership of their goals and actions. We want them to assume that their goals and actions can truly be accomplished by them, not for them.

   - Accountability: We want others to live the Harry S. Truman creed: The buck stops here. They must accept the notion that they reap the rewards and the consequences of attaining or not attaining their goals.

   - Buy-In: We know that none of this works unless everyone "buys in." People will not be committed unless they feel that they have been empowered and also have been considered in the process of establishing and managing the goals and strategies. "Do it the way I tell you, and shut up" may actually work (in only some cases) through fear and compliance, but it will not buy commitment (and often will breed underlying resentment).

——————— A Client's Story ———————

One of our clients was a fast-growing start-up company, a creator of software that helped their clients manage their own businesses. The founders had created a great new idea, and they and their employees were working very hard, moving at great speed to complete the activities necessary to grow the company at the high pace they desired.

This company was, in many ways, a typical technology start-up. It was staffed by high-achieving technical specialists, run by optimistic hard-working owners, and funded by investors with great expectations.

When describing the nature of his work, one of the owners stated that it was a bit like trying to fix a flat tire while going 60 miles an hour. What he meant was that he was trying to create all the systems and processes that would support his company now and in the future, while also meeting the needs and expectations of the fast-growing group of clients that needed attention right now. It was a business version of Whack a Mole—the team could hardly move fast enough.

As is also typical of such technology start-ups, frenetic activity is not always as productive as one would like. In fact people often work so fast and so hard in companies such as this, that they lose sight of the goals and how to reach them. They're doing lots of stuff each day, but it isn't always the right stuff. It's stuff only a hamster could love.

This company, led by its major owner and CEO, recognized that they "were lost in the weeds." While they were busy working hard to create business systems that would help their clients, they actually were in great need for a system that would help them manage and grow their own firm.

One of the most visible and immediate improvements they made involved the conduct of the meetings held by the management team. Whereas they used to conduct meetings that were rambling, long-winded, and unfocused, they now dealt with the *vital few* in an effective and conclusive manner.

The single most important means for doing that was to follow a very simple protocol at each meeting. They always posed this question to all the attendees at the very beginning of the meeting:

"WHAT ARE YOUR GOALS FOR THIS MEETING? IF OUR TIME TOGETHER TODAY IS SUCCESSFUL, WHAT WILL WE ACCOMPLISH?"

They had not started their previous meetings in this way, and as a consequence they often floundered, accomplishing little and walking away frustrated at the futility of meetings. Conversely, when they all focused on answering this question, they were forced to accomplish at least three things of great value.

First, they now focused immediately on defining their goals for the meeting. Thus, they defined what would make the meeting successful: accomplishing those goals. They were then compelled to conduct the meeting so that the goals would be met. After all, who wants to be a failure, especially when success is described so clearly and easily? Certainly not this group of high achievers. No rambling, no tangents in the discussions, no long-winded stories and excuses—just a strong focus on achieving the goals.

Second, they now could accomplish a great deal in a short amount of time. They were now highly focused on the goals, and how to achieve them, and they learned to ignore the *trivial many* other activities that merely distracted them.

Third, they could now begin a longer-term process of continually focusing on their goals, instead of just working hard each day at whatever came their way. This prompted them to think of new ways to accomplish their goals—ways that would not have even been considered previously.

This latter point is one of simple awareness—a deceptively powerful tool. For example, perhaps you remember when you last brought home a different car—whether a new model from the showroom or a used one. Then, as you drove around, you were amazed at the number of cars that looked like yours. They were, of course, out there all the time, just waiting for you to notice. So, too, it is in your business. Once you elevate your goals to become clear and important, you'll constantly find new ways to accomplish them. And so will everyone who works with you.

Let's summarize. You've empowered your team to achieve their goals, and you now want to create a system of managing that will keep them focused on goals all the time, provide them with clear guidelines, and reward them when goals are achieved. And you know that this system must rely upon clarity, effective communication, and commitment.

With this general framework in mind, we now turn to six specific tools that will assist you in creating an effective system of managing. All of these tools can be implemented easily and quickly.

THE GOAL MANAGEMENT TEAM (GMT)

—————————— Mike's Company ——————————

"Once I had established the framework for empowerment," says Mike, "I formed a group of my top managers to focus on our goals. I knew that I had the right people: I just needed to be specific with them about the goals that the company should accomplish and how we could make that happen.

"We call this group the Goal Management Team, or GMT. We call it this because the primary responsibility of this group is to ensure that we achieve our goals. Members of the GMT include:

- The head of the organization (in my company that's me, but it could be a department head in a larger organization).
- Those individuals who directly report to the head person.

"The key managers are not there to bring the head person up-to-date or to get his or her advice or approval. These are team meetings that are held to define the company's plans and goals, and to measure performance versus plan on a regular basis.

"This team of key managers deals only with the *vital few*, the most important things that affect their goals. This group does not get involved in what we term the *trivial many*, the little day-to-day things that often divert top management attention.

"The GMT is not a management-by-consensus decision-making body, nor is it a democratic body, like a board of directors, where the members vote on motions. Control in the GMT rests with the person accountable for his specific area of responsibility. The person responsible for the results defines the actions to be taken to achieve the goals. The other members of the GMT may provide counsel and advice, but it is the responsible person who makes the decisions about his area of responsibility."

Inherent in the intent of the GMT is that everyone's input can be valuable and even critical to the organization's success. Even those who might be considered to be ignorant of a specific topic or functional area may have valuable information or insights. In the end, the person responsible for that functional area will make the final decision, but it will be with a full consideration of all available information.

A True Story

In 1707, the British Fleet was engaged in battle with the French in the Mediterranean Sea. Returning home from a successful skirmish, Admiral Sir Clowdisley Showvell ran into thick fog near the coast of England. Unfortunately, this was anything but a simple inconvenience.

Sir Clowdisley and his contemporaries in the early 1700s were at a distinct disadvantage when it came to navigating the open seas: They never really knew where they were. They had, of course, no GPS or radios, and the navigation aids of the day were inadequate for determining position accurately. Although they were able to be reasonably accurate in determining their latitude (their north-south position), they had enormous difficulty in estimating their longitude (their east-west position).

In fact, it would be many decades until this problem was solved. In the meantime, Sir Clowdisley, like his fellow sailors, did his best to estimate his location, but it was not uncommon at that time to be many miles off course. This was a big deal if you were only a short distance away from a wave-battered and rocky coast. So it was for Sir Clowdisley.

Knowing that the situation was dicey, Sir Clowdisley summoned all his navigators to provide their opinions. The consensus was that they were safely west of the Brittany peninsula, off the west coast of France.

At the same time, one of the sailors on the crew approached Sir Clowdisley to admit that he had been estimating the fleet's location on his own during the passage and that he believed that the fleet was in grave danger. The sailor's admission was a brave act in itself, because the Royal Navy forbade an inferior from engaging in navigation exercises. (That was the domain of the navigators and officers.) Sir Clowdisley immediately had him hanged for mutiny.

Soon after, the fleet struck the Scilly Islands off the southwest tip of England. Approximately 2,000 men were lost.

We can't resist cautioning you against making Scilly decisions. But we're sure you get the point: Everybody is smarter than one person, and you want to be sure to consider all the available data. The GMT is designed to help you do that, while allowing—indeed compelling—each person to determine their desired course of action to achieve their goals.

THE SIX TOOLS

The GMT has six tools at its disposal to implement its management system and to achieve its goals through an empowerment framework. These are:

1. GMT meetings.
2. Team resourcing.
3. Position descriptions.
4. One-on-ones.
5. Daily huddles.
6. A company-wide reward program.

MANAGEMENT SYSTEM TOOLS

GMT Meetings

The GMT Meetings are held every month, as soon as the previous month's financial statements are ready. The GMT meetings are designed to:

- Define your company plans and goals.
- Measure and monitor your plan-versus-actual results.
- Create action steps to ensure goal achievement.

Note that the GMT meetings are not management-by-committee meetings, staff meetings, or meetings for the head of the organization to "hold court." These are team meetings that are focused on only six major topics in order to help the team achieve the organization's goals:

1. Planning.
2. Revenue generation.
3. Productivity.
4. Profitability.
5. Policies.
6. Strategies and actions to achieve goals.

The GMT meeting itself is tightly structured, while allowing great freedom of voice. Everyone is encouraged to provide insights and counsel, but each person is accountable for his own area of responsibility.

Every GMT meeting has an agenda, which addresses only those issues that fall under the six topics and which specifies the time required for each responsible person to address his topic. The agenda is provided to each GMT member two or three days in advance of the meeting, although last-minute items can be added at the meeting.

Every meeting involves three roles: a chairperson, a secretary, and a timekeeper. These roles may be permanent or they may be rotated among the members of the GMT.

The chairperson keeps the meeting on track by focusing everyone's attention on the agenda and the organization's goals. The chair also seeks to move the team closer to achieving its goals by creating action steps, which are composed of three parts:

- **A description of the specific action to be taken.**
- **The identification of the person responsible.**
- **A date for completion.**

In fact, the action steps from the previous meeting become agenda items for the next meeting. The chairperson directs each meeting to ensure that the action steps due that day have been completed.

The following table is a sample agenda. It shows dates for today's meeting and the two successive meetings, the three people involved in running the meeting, and the action steps for today and the future. It also shows the organization's goals, which should always be in front of everyone.

The agenda also has space for the goals for today's meeting. The Chair poses this question at the beginning of each GMT Meeting to ensure that she knows what to do to make this meeting a successful one: "What are your Goals for this meeting? If our time together today is successful, what will we accomplish?"

GMT Agenda and Action Items

Date Today:4/13/11 @ 9:00 a.m.	Chair: Ken	Sec: Noreen	T/K: John
Next Date: 5/10/11@ 9:00 a.m.	Chair:Noreen	Sec: John	T/K: Amy
Next Date: 6/9/11@ 9:00 a.m.	Chair: John	Sec: Amy	T/K:

OUR GOALS FOR THIS FISCAL YEAR

- Net Profit Before Tax and Rewards: 8%
- Customer Rating: 8.5 (out of 10)

What are our goals today? If our time together today is successful, what will we accomplish?

Time	#	ACTION ITEMS and AGENDA	Who?	When?
2	1	Set dates for next two GMT meetings and assign timekeeper 2 months out.	Chair	Every Meeting
5	2	What are our goals today? If our meeting is successful, what will we accomplish today?	Chair	Every Meeting
90	3	**Comparison of plan versus actual results for prior month and YTD, and creation of corrective action steps to achieve plan.**	GMT Members	Every Meeting
20	4	Create a plan to improve operational efficiencies in Residential Division	Doug	5/10/11
20	5	Create a marketing plan for new apartment division	Laurie	5/10/11

Was our meeting successful? Did we meet our goals?

The secretary records all the action steps generated in the meeting and provides these to the person who will be the chair for the next meeting. These new action steps will then become a part of the agenda for the meeting next time.

The timekeeper tracks the time for each topic and informs the Chair when time is out or nearly so. The Chair then decides if a minimal amount of time should be added to complete the topic or if the topic should be taken off line. The intent here is not to extend the meeting, but rather to make it as efficient as possible in addressing the topics in a timely manner.

Mike's Company

"Now we're ready for a critical topic for the Goal Management Team: the comparison of our company goals to our actual performance. We monitor this for each month and for the year to date.

"This means that we have created a plan for the year on a monthly basis; we have goals for each month. In our company, we have goals for profitability and for our customer survey. Let's look at the profitability goal as an example of the analysis process.

"In the following table is a simplified version of what each GMT member receives from our financial department. They get this before the GMT meeting, with the actual numbers filled in, so that they have time to analyze their department results and formulate their action steps before the meeting.

Plan versus Actual Financial Performance

	THIS MONTH				YEAR TO DATE				
	Plan $	% Sales	Actual $	% Sales	Variance $	Plan $	% Sales	Actual $	% Sales	Variance $
Net Sales									
COGS									
Gross Profit									
S&M Expenses									
Adjusted Gross Profit									
G&A Expenses									
Net Operating Profit									
Other Expense/Income									
NP before tax and rewards									
Rewards									
NPBT									

COGS: Cost of Goods Sold
S&M: Sales and Marketing expenses, including salaries
G&A: General and Administrative expenses (Overhead)

NP: Net Profit
NPBT: Net Profit before Taxes
% Sales: Net Sales equals 100%, other items are calculated as a percentage of net sales

"When we hold our GMT meetings, we first look at the overall company performance, which is represented by this table. You'll notice that the vertical listing on the left side of the table is really an income statement. Because one of our goals is 8% net profit before taxes, the income statement presented here is the best way to track our progress for this goal.

"Using the information in this table, we compare our actual performance to our goals for the current month and for the year to date. You can see that we express the actual performance both in dollars and as a percentage. Both of these numbers are very helpful to us.

"If our performance is on plan or ahead of plan, we discuss the reasons. We do this so that we can ensure that we can sustain this level of performance. We want to know what we're doing right, so that we can keep on doing it.

"If our performance is behind plan, we also discuss the reasons, but only to learn lessons about where we fell short. We don't spend any real time rehashing old news. Our focus is much more heavily directed toward the creation of action steps to get us back on plan. In fact, we won't move from this agenda item until we have a 'plan to get back on plan.'

"This discussion of plan versus actual performance involves each department, the heads of which briefly discuss what they will do to sustain good performance or what action steps they will conduct to get back on plan. And each manager is responsible for these numbers; they cannot expect the financial person to present and explain the numbers for their department. This is a key point: Each manager is responsible and accountable for the performance of their group and for the actions needed to meet their goals.

"Now, don't forget that we have another goal in our company. We want to score a minimum 8.5 on a scale of 10 in our customer satisfaction surveys. Our discussions on this goal would be similar to what I've just described. We'd compare plan with actual, discuss our successes or shortcomings, and create action steps as needed.

"And so the meeting would progress, from topic to topic. Ken would direct the discussions to ensure that each item was completed successfully. If this were not the case, he would ask the responsible person to describe the corrective action they intend to take to get back on plan. This would include a date as well as a specific description.

"Then, Ken asks the question "Did we meet our goals for today? Was our meeting successful?" Everyone is encouraged to provide an answer to this. If the meeting goals were not met (which shouldn't occur if the meeting were well run), Ken should ensure that a specific action step be re-addressed or that some action step be created to address the issue outside of the meeting, by some specific date."

Team Resourcing

The second tool in the management system is team resourcing. This is used when the person responsible for an action step, or some other specific activity, finds difficulty in accomplishing that activity. They need help, they need more resources, which the team will provide to them.

For example, let's assume that there is a productivity issue related to a large project being run by Doug. He's not sure that he knows how to solve the issue on his own.

Consequently, he calls for team resourcing. This is a very powerful tool, when used correctly, and that means that Doug will follow some very specific ground rules.

Team Resourcing Ground Rules

- The person responsible for the problem activity facilitates the team resourcing.

- The facilitator chooses a timekeeper and chooses the time to be allotted (for example, "I need 10 minutes for team resourcing for this issue").

- The facilitator defines the *apparent problem* and gives the background and facts.

- The facilitator then asks *"What's the goal?"* which the group helps answer.

- The facilitator asks someone to record all the suggestions that will be made.

- Everyone agrees to be open to all suggestions—no ideas are rejected.

- The facilitator then asks the group for ideas on how the goal can be attained.

- The facilitator encourages balanced participation, with **no** negative editorializing allowed and **no** discussions, only succinct suggestions.

- The facilitator creates corrective actions to be taken after the Team Resourcing is completed.

There are two very important attributes to team resourcing. We think that they are the real reasons for the success of this tool.

First, we distinguish clearly between the apparent problem and the goal, because it's too easy to solve an immediate problem and still not accomplish the goal. For example, low productivity is Doug's apparent problem. But it may be that the goal is not just to push for project-specific productivity but to build a crew that is loyal and dedicated and will provide high productivity for every job over the long term. And this goal likely will provoke a different set of suggestions and action steps than attempting to solve Doug's immediate problem.

Second, everyone is encouraged to participate, because everyone is smarter than one person. So, the rules are quite strict about not allowing strongly opinionated folks to squelch the flow of ideas. When the exercise is underway, everyone just calls out their ideas of what might help to accomplish the goals. The scribe writes down the ideas for all to see, and no one is allowed to provide negative comments about anyone's ideas, as absurd as they may sound at the time. Nor is anyone allowed to start a discussion, lecture, or debate. It's just a rapid-fire series of suggestions from everyone involved.

This is done so that everyone will contribute and because even seemingly-absurd ideas sometimes can be directly useful or can cause others to think of something that is valuable. It's this "hitchhiking" of ideas that often gives team resourcing its real power.

When completed successfully, team resourcing provides the facilitator with new ideas—new resources. But this is not a democratic exercise; the issue isn't settled with a popular vote. The person who called for the team resourcing exercise, the person empowered to be responsible and accountable for his department and his actions, is free to choose among the new resources to create successful action plans. The decision is his.

Position descriptions

The position description is the third tool in the management system. Although we discussed this when we described the empowerment structure, we want to emphasize here the importance of this tool for providing everyone with clarity on their goals and responsibilities.

There are two parts to the position description that are especially useful to the management system: goals and authority. These two items should provide a clear understanding between manager and team member regarding desired outcomes and certain boundaries.

The **goals** of the position define the major criteria for success. If the person in the position accomplishes the goals, they generally will be successful in the position.

The **authority** section of the position description outlines the limits to the authority for the person in the position. Usually, these relate to something such as spending and contractual limits. For example, the position may carry the authority to spend up to $1,000, outside of budgeted funds per quarter, for discretionary items. Similarly, the person in the position might have the authority to contract with a new customer for up to $50,000.

In this authority section, the position description helps to define the boundaries required for you to create an effective empowerment structure. The position description makes it clear where the boundaries exist, making everyone's life easy, because it brings clarity and avoids ambiguity.

One-on-ones

The fourth tool in the management system is a discussion between manager and staff called the one-on-one. These are regular meetings, perhaps as frequently as weekly depending upon circumstances, to ensure that goals will be achieved. They should take no more than five to 10 minutes (they're not designed as a general discussion forum), but they're a very powerful goal-focused tool.

The one-on-ones are intended to keep everyone focused on their goals, and they are conducted in an informal yet structured way. For every one-on-one, there are five questions that should be convincingly answered by the team member. You can ask the questions in your own words, but here they are:

- Did you achieve your goals since we last spoke?
  - If not, what corrective action will you take to get back on plan?
  - If you did, what will you do to stay at this high level of achievement?
- What are your goals for the coming period?
- Are there any obstacles in your way?
- What will we do to remove the obstacles?

You'll notice that the last question involves "we." The action step taken here is an agreement between the manager and employee as to what will be done to remove any barriers to success. If the barriers are removed, the manager should expect the goals to be achieved.

The daily huddle

The fifth tool in the management system is the daily huddle. This is an informal discussion between the manager and the team regarding the activities that will need to be completed in the upcoming period.

Depending upon the nature of your organization, you might decide to have a huddle daily, weekly, or even monthly. If you are in a very fast-moving environment (one in which activities change significantly from one day to the next), you'll benefit from doing this daily.

The daily huddle is intended to bring clarity and agreement to the team regarding the upcoming activities. It's also intended to reinforce the positive things that have happened since the last huddle. We believe that reinforcing positive activities is a powerful morale booster in any situation.

The Daily Huddle

FOOTBALL, CONSTRUCTION, AND THE BLUE ANGELS

What do football teams, construction companies, and the Blue Angels all have in common? They all have a brief but critical meeting just before they go out to execute their activities.

Football teams have a huddle before every play. They do this because every play is important—it's a potential scoring play—and because conditions change between each play.

Similarly, construction companies have a morning project meeting. They do this because each day is filled with numerous activities that demand attention to detail and close coordination of resources, and because conditions likely will change from one day to the next.

The Blue Angels have a pre-flight briefing before every flight. They do this because the weather and other conditions are different for every flight and because the pilots' lives depend upon virtually flawless execution every time.

WHAT'S IN THIS FOR YOU?

Remember the Paul Newman movie *Cool Hand Luke*? One of the memorable lines in this movie is "what we have here is a failure to communicate."

The daily huddle is designed for situations that require close communication, usually on a regular or recurring basis. For example, it is useful in coordinating many activities between sales and purchasing, sales and operations, and sales and accounting. There are countless other applications.

The daily huddle focuses on the goals for the upcoming period (whether today or this week). It also includes a clear understanding of the activities required by each attendee of the meeting, and an agreement on the date for completion of these activities. In other words, it includes Action Steps.

The daily huddle often works best in the morning, when the day is about to start, but this may not be the case for your situation. You may choose to use it daily or even only once a week, depending upon the circumstances. If you want to call it the weekly huddle, that's just fine.

One last thing: We like to start the daily huddle on a positive note, because we think that positive affirmation brings a sense of high morale and accomplishment.

So, when you hold this Huddle, let everyone take one minute to discuss the "Team Wins" that have occurred since the last huddle. Bathe yourselves in good news, and focus on replicating it.

So, here's the agenda for your daily huddle:

- What were our wins for the last period?
- What are our goals for the upcoming period?
- What are the action steps we'll complete to achieve those goals?

A company-wide reward program

The sixth tool in the management system is a company-wide reward program. We like to see a direct link between the company goals and the successful efforts of everyone in the company in achieving those goals. When the goals are achieved, we like to see everyone receive a reward.

We use the term *reward* purposely, because we want everyone to see a direct link between the attainment of a goal and some form of reward. Though there is controversy as to whether money provides an incentive to all employees (it certainly does to many), and although "bonuses" are often based upon discretionary criteria ("If we have a good year, trust me, I'll take care of you"), a reward provides clear and tangible evidence of success ("If we make our goals, every employee will get the following...").

The reward program is designed to accomplish several objectives. All are critical to the success of the firm in attaining its goals.

First, it is designed to reward the entire team for their accomplishments in achieving your company goals. Because you set those goals with a purpose, you convey to your employees that the goals are important. When the team accomplishes the goals, they have all achieved something important—something that deserves a reward.

Second, it is designed to link directly with your "plan versus actual" exercise. You monitor and manage the performance of the company in order to ensure that you will attain the goals. By having clear, unambiguous goals, and by monitoring results monthly, at minimum, everyone will be aware of the organization's progress toward achieving the goals. If the company lags in performance, everyone will be expected to help create action steps to get back on track.

Third, it "keeps everyone's head in the game." By rewarding achievements on a relatively frequent schedule (such as quarterly), you create a score-keeping mentality—a culture that values frequent monitoring and regular links between achievement and rewards. This, in turn, invests the program with importance and immediacy.

Fourth, in our experience, people like to have goals. They want to know what they should do to achieve success. They also want tools and coaching on how to attain the goals, and they simply appreciate being rewarded when they do.

The company goals

The reward program is based upon the company goals, which should represent vital issues necessary for the survival and success of the firm. For example, assume that your company has two goals for the current year:

- **Net profit before tax of $5 million**
- **A customer survey score of 8.5 on a scale of 0 to 10.**

Next, you must be very clear about their attainment. First, both of the goals listed must be attained in order for the company to pay a reward. Keeping customers happy is not enough if you can't make a profit, and making a profit without maintaining a satisfied customer base is also inadequate. Second, the numbers listed for each goal must be attained; there is no reward for getting close, nor is there a pro rata payout for the reward based upon getting close.

We like the goals to be measured often in order to keep an updated status. Consequently, goals that are established on a quarterly or even monthly basis bring an immediacy and urgency to all the employees. Note that each month's goals may differ, depending upon factors such as the seasonality or cyclicality of the business.

Available reward money

Before any reward money is paid to employees, you must decide the total amount that is available for company-wide rewards. Allowing for capital requirements, retirement of debt, dividends, retained earnings, and other items, you will determine the size of the available reward pool for the employees, if the goals are attained.

As an example, our clients often have paid a reward of 7 to 25% of salary to their employees when the company goals are attained. Some have created a reward system that literally has no upper boundary in terms of total dollars paid. As the company does better so too do the employees. It's up to you; just be very clear about the ground rules.

The payout

The reward will be paid, if earned, after the end of each quarter or each month. To ensure that the firm makes its goals over the long haul, the quarterly rewards might start out modestly and then progress more aggressively.

For example, the firm may decide to pay 10 percent of the potential year-long reward in the first quarter, 15 percent in the second quarter, 25 percent in the third quarter, and 50 percent in the last quarter. Though you may adjust these percentages as you see fit, "backloading" the program like this ensures that an inordinate amount of money is not paid for early goal attainment, even if the final year-long goal is not attained. This is designed to encourage year-long attainment of the goals and a concerted effort to improve long term performance.

Should we also reward individual performance?

Whether the company attains its goals or not, there likely will be individuals who will exhibit a high level of personal achievement. Shouldn't these individuals be rewarded?

We love to see high-achieving individuals rewarded. But our first loyalty is to the overall success of the company. Remember the fable of the Golden Goose? As long as the Golden Goose was healthy, it produced golden eggs. The first priority is the health of the goose.

So, too, is the first priority the health, or success, of the company. When the company is healthy, we have the means to reward everyone. So, we like to see the first and major reward based upon achieving the company goals, thus helping create a culture where everyone works together to do so.

However, we also always want to encourage our high-performing people, so we like them to have a reward for achieving their individual goals. As a general rule, we like this reward to be less than the reward that can be earned from achieving the company goal. For example, if an employee might earn $10,000 when the company achieves its goals, she might also earn an additional reward for achieving her individual goals, but this would be something less than $10,000.

The notion here is that the company goals are paramount. When the company is successful, everyone shares in the success because everyone contributed to this success.

A Client's Story

R emember Royal Robbins, the big-rock wall climber we told you about in the opening chapter? Royal and his wife, Liz, were clients of ours many years ago. They had decided that they needed some assistance in turning their company into a great one.

When we began working with them and their team, there was some bald skepticism among some of the managers. The company had tried various "programs" before, and none had really panned out successfully. One of the vice presidents of the company surprised all of us when he stated, "We've never come close to achieving goals like this. If we make these goals I'll wear a tutu to the office for an entire day."

Whether this was the primary incentive and motivator for the rest of the management team is debatable, but we have photographs of that manager in his pink tutu, smiling away because the company did indeed reach its goals. And Royal and Liz Robbins also smiled as they gave out reward checks to every employee.

A similar story took place with another of our clients. At an early GMT meeting we outlined the goals that we believed the company could achieve for the coming year, and the CEO responded, "That would be amazing to do." We asked the CEO at that GMT meeting, "If your Goal Management Team accomplished these goals, would you take the team and their spouses on a Carnival cruise to Nassau and give all the employees a percentage reward?" He said, "It would certainly be worth that—so, yes!" The team achieved the goals, and everyone went on that Carnival cruise, first class!

In both of these cases, as well as in many others, it was the ingenuity, creativity, enthusiasm, and hard work of the GMT members and the members of their teams that made this happen. They created and executed the strategies that achieved these ambitious, and perhaps seemingly impossible, goals. And they reaped the rewards.

This stuff isn't magic. It's the *6 Habits of Highly Successful Managers*. You can do it with your group or company, and we hope you will. It works.

Points to Remember

- An effective management system combines:
  - Clarity.
  - Communication.
  - Commitment.
    - Responsibility.
    - Accountability.
    - Buy-in.
- The Goal Management Team (GMT) has responsibility for achieving the company goals, and has six key tools at its disposal:
  - GMT meetings.
  - Team resourcing.
  - Position descriptions.
  - One-on-ones.
  - Daily huddle.
  - Company-wide reward program.
- The GMT meeting is a key tool for managing actual achievement relative to the plans and goals.
  - Define the company plans and goals.
  - Measure and monitor plan versus actual results.
  - Create action steps to ensure achievement of goals.
- Team resourcing harnesses the wisdom of the group to provide managers with new ideas to achieve their goals.

Using your financial statements to generate more profit and more cash

What can you do to make more profit?

Determining how to increase profits in your company is, of course, a long-term and dedicated exercise. But we want to give you four areas for focus, and also provide you with one of the best tools we know to gain immediate increases in your profitability.

General ways

There four ways to increase profitability in your company. All are within your control, and you should be considering all four of them on a regular basis:

1. Raise prices.
2. Sell more stuff.
3. Reduce overhead.
4. Reduce Cost of Goods Sold (COGS).

We advise you, of course, to employ all four of these tactics. If you can raise prices and sell more products and services, you'll make more profits right away. And if you can reduce your overhead, you'll build a more lean and efficient business.

Reducing your Cost of Goods Sold is also a very useful tactic, and you can do this by getting lower prices from your suppliers. One of the best ways to get these lower prices is to ask your suppliers for discounts.

Taking discounts

We always advise our clients to take advantage of vendor discount terms. It's one of the best deals out there. But why is this so, and why should a business offer these terms to its customers?

Businesses offer discounts to their customers in order to receive payment sooner than by using standard payment terms. By offering such a discount, the business accepts a lower amount for its products in exchange for earlier payment.

For example, to obtain payment sooner, the business might offer discount terms, such as 2 percent 10, net 30. In this case, the customer has two choices. One choice is to pay in 30 days—that is, net 30—just as in commonly used standard terms. The second choice is to take the discount and pay 2 percent less than the full amount, but to make this payment within 10 days of the invoice date.

There are trade-offs for taking discounts for both the business and the customer. Let's look at an example to assess the value of these trade-offs.

Let's assume that the customer has an invoice for $100, and that she has been offered discount terms of 2 percent 10, net 30. This gives her two choices for payment, and we'll look at both choices, as shown in the following diagram.

The Math of Taking Discounts

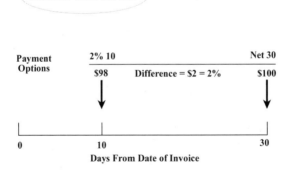

If the customer takes the discount, she pays $98 (2 percent less, or $2 less, than the full amount of $100). And she pays this amount by the *10th day from the invoice date.*

If the customer chooses not to take the discount she pays the full amount of $100. And she pays this by the *30th day from the invoice date.*

So, does it make sense for the customer to take advantage of the discount? Does it make sense for the business to offer the discount? Let's look this from both perspectives.

For the customer taking the discount, she pays $2 less, or 2 percent less, than the full amount. By paying in 10 days instead of 30, she gains $2. And she gains this $2, or 2 percent, by moving her payment up by 20 days, from day 30 to day 10.

So, she has a gain of 2 percent in a 20 day period of time. Let's see what this means on a yearly basis.

2 percent gain for a 20 day period

365/20 = 18.25   20-day periods in a year, each worth 2 percent

$$18.25$$
$$\underline{\text{x 2 percent}}$$
36.5 percent annual gain

In other words, by taking the discount, she made use of a transaction that paid her the equivalent of 36.5 percent a year! There aren't many places that a business owner can find that kind of return.

This customer, however, like many of our clients, might tell us that she doesn't have enough cash on hand to take the discount. This calculation shows us that as long as she could borrow money for less than 36.5 percent, it would be worthwhile to take the discount.

What about the business that offered the discount? Why would they make such a good deal for the customer?

Businesses generally offer discount terms to obtain cash more quickly. They also may offer discount terms to better ensure that they will be paid at all. This is especially true in tough economic times when customer payments can move from net 30 to net never. In either case, the business is willing to forego some profit (they are obtaining less revenue by offering the discount) in exchange for the quick receipt of cash.

So, the trade-offs for the customer and the business are opposite and related. In many cases, however, it is advantageous for both parties to employ discount terms.

For the customer taking the discount, she pays less money for the product, but she must pay sooner. She also will enjoy a higher profit in her business (because the discount lowered her cost of goods, her profitability will go up). Even if she has to borrow money to take the discount, she will make money if she can borrow for less than 36.5 percent.

For the business offering the discount, it will receive cash quickly. This will satisfy its need for immediate cash or for assurance of complete payment in a timely manner. In exchange, the business will accept 2 percent less for its product.

We advise our clients to take vendor discounts whenever they are offered—always. Our advice to clients that may offer a discount to *their* customers is to offer discounts only when cash is needed quickly or when it is important to ensure timely and complete collections.

What can you do to get more cash?

Business owners know that when the business makes a profit, it does not always have lots of cash. There might even be a deficit; while making a profit for the month, the business can still be short of cash. This is annoying, and, to some owners, somewhat mysterious.

Oftentimes, however, there is a solution to this problem. It is within the control of the business and is relatively easy to accomplish.

But first, let's look at the general ways that an owner can get cash in the business; there are four of them. They're all under the owner's control, although some are easier to accomplish than others.

First, the owner can put more of her personal funds into the business. But when we talk with owners about this option, they balk. They tell us, "You don't get it. The idea is for me to take money out of my business, not put it in." Good point.

Second, the owner can obtain a loan. Indeed, this is a useful option in many cases, and banks have made a good living for centuries by providing the money. Unfortunately for the business owner, the money must be paid back, together with the interest attached to the loan.

Third, the company can make more profit. In many cases, though not all, making more profit can generate more cash for the business. But usually, the amount of additional profit that a company can make, by working just a little harder say, is not sufficient to make a real difference.

And in many cases, the business can actually have less cash when it generates more profit. For example, this commonly occurs when a company must buy products in advance of sales (must carry inventory) or when it must wait for its customers to pay for the services or goods that it purchases (when customers are "on credit").

Why is that so? Remember: The company is required to buy the inventory it hopes to sell at some future date, and it also must pay its workers every day. These expenses are a cash drain for the company until the money from a sale is actually collected from the customer. So, the company spends money for inventory and internal expenses, but it doesn't get that money back until the customer sends payment, which can be months after the company paid for the goods and labor. Thus, for the company, the higher the sales, the lower the cash flow.

This leads us to the fourth way to make more cash, and that is to operate the company more efficiently. This is the one place that the owner can see relatively significant effects upon cash flow, with relatively little cost or effort.

We'll talk here about two ways for doing this: decreasing inventory and decreasing accounts receivable. We'll show you how you can determine what these mean to you, in real dollars.

Not every business has inventory or accounts receivable. Service businesses, such as accounting firms or consulting engineers, sell their time rather than a tangible product and don't carry inventory. Other businesses, such as retailers, collect money at the time of the sale. If that is your case, you needn't worry about the effects of inventory or accounts receivable on your cash flow. Good for you—that's just one less thing to create worry, and you've got enough of those.

Managing inventory

Let's look first at companies that sell tangible products and for which inventory is an important part of the business. Managing that inventory is a high-level skill. Too little inventory results in lost sales and a furious and frustrated sales force, whereas too much inventory ties up large quantities of cash and may put the business in a precarious financial position. Thus, the person who manages the inventory has the head of sales on one side and the financial officer on the other side reminding him of what he should do.

In short, every dollar of your inventory is a dollar that you no longer have in cash. But you know that you need inventory. It's the "stuff" that customers come to buy. No stuff, no sale. And sometimes, if we don't have the stuff on hand, the customer leaves to shop where they have stuff.

Our experiences indicate that the most common problem related to inventory is that businesses usually carry too much of it. Sure, there are firms that have too little inventory (those are the "backorders" and "stock out" notices you get), and there are those who do a masterful job of balancing the need for sales and cash flow. Good for them.

For most firms, however, that is not the case. These companies need to focus on how to reduce their excess inventory and get cash back into the business. Fortunately, this can actually be done.

A trick done with mirrors

Let's look at a fictitious company that sells bicycles to see how it might manage its inventory. We're going to be looking at two things here: the value of the inventory, and the average time it takes to sell that quantity of inventory.

First we examine their balance sheet (bicycles are an asset, and assets are found on the balance sheet), and we find that the value of the company's inventory of bicycles is $5,000,000.

$$\text{Value of Inventory} = \$5,000,000$$

Next, we calculate how long it takes to sell this amount of inventory. To do this, we look on the annual income statement at the line called "Cost of Goods Sold, Materials." (We look only at the materials portion of cost of goods sold (COGS); direct labor is not part of this calculation.) We find that this totals $10,000,000.

$$\text{Value of Materials Portion of COGS} = \$10,000,000$$

Now we perform this simple division: $\dfrac{\$10,000,000}{\$5,000,000} = 2 \text{ "turns"}$

Accountants would say that the company's inventory is "turning two times." In other words, during the year, the company must sell twice the value of this inventory to equal the value of the materials portion of the cost of goods sold for the year.

So what? We agree, that's not too meaningful. Let's make this easier to use.

$$\frac{365 \text{ days/year}}{2 \text{ turns/year}} \quad = \quad 183 \text{ days/turn}$$

This number, called Inventory Days, tells us that, on average, it takes the firm 183 days to sell its inventory—to turn it over one time. Let's see what this means on a daily basis.

$$\frac{\$5,000,000}{183 \text{ days}} \quad = \quad \$27,322/\text{day}$$

This last calculation is a powerful one. It tells us that, on average, for every day that we could reduce Inventory Days in this company, we'd have $27,322 more cash!

You can do the same calculation for your company. Just follow the steps. We think you'll be surprised at how much a day's worth of inventory is in real cash.

But inventory is boring. I like to do the fun stuff!

Most CEOs and presidents don't get involved with inventory. They're usually off creating strategic initiatives, reviewing the "big picture" financial performance of the firm, or doing other such presidential things.

But there's big money to be found in that inventory. Imagine in the previous example that the firm had debts totaling $270,000. By lowering Inventory Days by 10, from 183 to 173, it could have enough available cash to erase that debt, and the annual interest payments that go with it. And now it could use that freed-up debt capacity for something else, like one of those strategic initiatives.

We have often seen companies that fit this profile closely. Their debts have been equal to their excess inventories, and when they got their inventory in line, they paid off the debt. It's like Christmas coming early.

Make no mistake about it: Managing inventory is tough stuff. But take the first step: *focus* on managing it. Even a reduction of a day or two can result in much-needed cash.

Accounts receivable

We can get a clue about the role of accounts receivable in creating a lack of cash flow when we consider the meaning of the term. An account receivable is a promise from a customer that you will be paid for the goods or services you provided. But you don't have the money yet; you'll get it, hopefully, some day in the future.

Meanwhile, as was the case with inventory, you had to pay all your expenses, with your cash, every day. Until you actually get payments from your customers, you'll be cash poor.

Let's determine how valuable these accounts receivable are to your cash position. We'll do a calculation similar to the one we did for inventory. And once again, we'll use one item from the income statement, revenues, and one item from the balance sheet, accounts receivable.

Another trick done with mirrors

Let's assume that the company had annual revenues of $20,000,000. And let's also assume that it had accounts receivable of $4,000,000.

$$\text{Annual revenues} = \$20,000,000$$

$$\text{Accounts Receivable (A/R)} = \$4,000,000$$

We can now do a calculation similar to the one we did for inventory

$$\frac{\$20,000,000}{\$4,000,000} = 5 \text{ “turns”}$$

Accountants would say that the company's accounts receivable is "turning five times." In other words, during the year, the company must collect five times the value of the accounts receivable to equal the value of the annual revenues.

Once again, we can almost hear you saying, "So what?" And once again, we agree. Let's try to put this in a form that makes some sense.

$$\frac{365 \text{ days/year}}{5 \text{ turns/year}} = 73 \text{ days/turn}$$

This number, called A/R Days, or Days Sales Outstanding (DSO) tells us that, on average, it takes the firm 73 days to collect its accounts receivable. Let's see what this means on a daily basis.

$$\frac{\$4,000,000}{73 \text{ days}} = \$54,795/\text{day}$$

Once again, this last calculation is a powerful one. It tells us that, on average, for every day that we could decrease A/R Days in this company, we'd have $54,795 more cash!

Though the figures we used here are fictitious, they do bear great resemblance to many of the firms we've known. It is not unusual for companies to have 60+ in A/R Days. This is an enormous waste of cash, and often results in the acquisition of loans to provide the company with the cash it needs to operate.

Let's assume here that the company's terms are net 30. It expects its customers to pay within 30 days of the invoice date. Let's see how much cash it could generate if it collected on time.

Company Terms	=	net 30
A/R Days	=	73 days
Difference	=	43 days (73-30)

So far, then, we've determined that the company's customers are taking 43 days "too long" to make payment. The management team has perhaps been so focused on sales that it has taken its eye off the A/R ball. This is very common.

Now, we know that for every day that A/R Days could be reduced, on average, the company would gain $54,795 in cash. Let's see what 43 days is worth.

$$43 \text{ days X } \$54,795 = \$2,356,164$$

Almost unbelievably, we've found a way to generate well more than two million dollars in cash for this company. All we have to do is get the customers to pay on time. Simple, huh?

Well, actually, it's not. These customers have gotten used to paying late. They'll be shocked, and probably offended, if we notify them suddenly that now we expect to be paid on time. We've helped to create their bad habit by not enforcing our own rules.

But we could, over time, reel them in to something close to our net 30, maybe even all the way. The first step is to gain a few days, and that is relatively easy.

One of the hidden dangers of letting A/R stretch out too long is that it empowers some weaker customers to neglect paying us at all. By the time we decide to chase them down for payment, they've become emboldened, or unable, to make the payment. Net 30 then becomes net never.

The trick here is to remember that your transaction with your customer is an agreement. You provide the goods or services, and the customer pays you. You never need to apologize for expecting to be paid on time. It's part of the agreement.

Once again, please do these calculations for your company. Just follow the steps. And learn to collect your payments on time. You'll greatly increase your cash flow, in one of the easiest ways we know.

Points to Remember

Monitoring and managing your business is a key to success, and your financial statements are your scorecards. Understand what you want to know from your financial statements, make a profit plan and cash flow plan for each month of the year, ask your accountant to provide you with the information, and then take the necessary corrective actions to achieve the goals you've set in your plans.

Simple, huh?

Business plan outline and guidance

How to use this outline

There are many uses for a business plan, including:

- Informing the employees about the goals and strategies of the company.
- Planning for major expansions or new locations.
- Raising money from investors or securing a major loan.
- Preparing to sell the company.

The outline here can be used for all of these applications. The depth of information and the emphasis will vary, however, depending upon the circumstances.

For example, when the plan is developed for the employees, it serves as a cookbook for the goals, strategies, and operational tactics that will be used over the coming period, say the next year. In this case, there should be high emphasis on the clarity of the strategies and the operational tactics used by each major department.

Conversely, when the plan is developed to obtain financing or a loan, there should be high emphasis on the financial plan. The bank will be less interested in the departmental operational tactics.

The information in the outline includes annotations about the content of key sections of the plan. Also included are some questions pertaining to those sections. The answers to these questions will help you complete the sections. It's not necessary to answer all the questions in each section, but you'll understand what's needed by reading all the questions.

The formulation of the business plan should focus on the company's goals and strategies. The goals state what the company intends to accomplish (for example, attain $2 million in net profit) and the strategies describe how this will be accomplished. As shown in the Business Planning Map that follows the outline, all of the information collection and analysis activities are a prelude to the creation of the company's goals and strategies.

You may be a bit overwhelmed by the thought of writing an entire business plan, especially if you don't like to write. There are, of course, some options available to you, such as using a good writer to help or finding a way to minimize the writing.

We like the second option. The Business Plan should be as short as possible—most people don't want to read pages and pages of prose. In fact, you should feel free to format your plan in bullet or outline form if you can describe the ideas clearly and comprehensively. This is especially applicable when the plan will be used for internal purposes.

And remember: The process is more important than the product. You should strive to create a company culture that emphasizes the need for constant planning and for the involvement of many of your team members.

Business Plan Outline

1. Purpose

2. Executive summary

3. The company
   A. Vision
   B. Mission
   C. History
   D. Current status
   E. Competitive advantages and disadvantages

4. Marketing plan
   A. Market and industry analysis
   B. Market segments
   C. Competitive environment
   D. Positioning
   E. Key customers
   F. Market opportunities

    G. Target markets

    H. Marketing strategies and goals

    I.   Resources needed and milestones

    J. Sales forecast

    K. Customer service

5. Operational plan

    A. Operational goals and strategies

    B. Management team and organizational chart

    C. Implementation plans

    D. Risks

6. Legal and professional issues

7. Financial plan

    A. Historical financial statements

    B. Pro formas

    C. Ratio analyses

    D. Sources and uses of funds

The Business Planning Map

1. Purpose

This section describes why you've written the business plan, whether for internal purposes (so that you can better manage the business), to obtain capital for growth, to outline the business' feasibility, or for some other reason. This can be done in a single paragraph.

2. Executive summary

This section summarizes the entire plan in two pages. Use tables and graphics to make it readable and compelling. Many outsiders will only read this section, so make it clear. If done well, it will lead the reader into the rest of the document. Complete the executive summary last—summarize from the detailed work that you put into the entire plan.

───────────── **Helpful Questions** ─────────────

- What is creating customer demand:
  - Industry wide?
  - For your products and services?
- How long will this persist and why?
- What opportunities does this create for you?
- What are your goals and general strategies?
- What's "the payoff"?
  - When will investors/lenders/owners get rewarded/paid back?
  - Why is this worth their while?

3. The company

A. Vision

This describes the very long-range goals for the company—<u>what it aspires to be</u> in the future. It should describe how the company will be better in some measurable way than it is now, will serve customers in a significant way, and will provide a great working environment for all the employees.

B. Mission statement

This describes, in a sentence or two, why the company exists—<u>what it does</u> in order to reach its vision. If the company executes on its mission over time, it will move closer to fulfilling its vision. Ideally, the company always operates within its mission.

C. History

This section describes the history of the company, highlighting events that are important to understanding the firm today. The whole section can be done in a page or less, in most cases.

D. Current status

This describes the business today, including its products, services, markets, management, and structure. It describes the strengths and weaknesses of the organization, and it probably can be done in a couple of pages.

E. Competitive advantages and disadvantages

This section tells why the company is special. Think hard about this. It's the description of why you'll be successful in the future. Also, describe frankly the company's weaknesses. Don't kid yourself here.

Helpful Questions

Products and Services
- What is special or even unique about your products/services?
- How long will this uniqueness last?
- How do the benefits you provide to customers differentiate your firm?
- Which offerings are viewed by customers as superior or inferior?

Markets
- What advantages do your markets (your buyers) provide you?
- What future advantages will the markets bring to you?

Marketing and Sales
- Are your sales and marketing capabilities superior/inferior and why?

- Do you have special customers and why?
- Do you have special distribution channels?
- What are your reputation and image?
- What are your costs and prices relative to the competition?

Operations and Finance
- How does your financial position give you an advantage or disadvantage?
- Do you have privileged relationships with suppliers?
- How capable are your vendors and your organizational structure?
- Do you have the ability to grow the company?
- What is the company's ability to adapt to new situations?
- Do you have the right equipment, people, and other assets?

4. Marketing plan

A. Market and industry analysis

This summarizes the characteristics and activities of all the industries in which you operate. You might wish to use graphics to illustrate the trends and growth in the market. Describe the forces that create demand in the industry, as well as current trends, with emphasis on how that affects your business.

Helpful Questions

- What key factors influence growth in your industry?
- What are the barriers to entry or exit?
- What are the distribution channels. (How do providers get to the customers?)
- What constraints to industry growth are there?
- What is the total size of the industry and the segments in which you operate, and what are the growth prospects?

B. Market segments

This section describes the groups of customers that you serve that are similar in their buying or usage behavior of your products or services. Also identify the relative importance of each segment.

―――――――――― Helpful Questions ――――――――――

- Are there groups of firms within your industry with similar characteristics, that is, with the same type of:
    - Customers (for example, retail versus wholesale)?
    - Product or service (for example, computer hardware versus software)?
    - Distribution channels (for example, work through architects versus directly)?
- Are there well-acknowledged segments already identified?
    - By an association or trade group?
    - By government classification code?
    - By business or trade press?
- Why are certain of these segments favorable or unfavorable to your organization?

C. Competitive environment

Describe, in detail, the competitive environment in which you operate. Remember to determine this: Why do people go to *them* (your competitors) instead of to you? It's probably some variation of price, quality, and service. Describe the strengths and weaknesses of each competitor and how they behave in the marketplace (for example, highly aggressive on price). Remember, too, that competition can come in various forms, including substitute products as well as new companies.

―――――――――― Helpful Questions ――――――――――

- Who are your competitors?
    - Provides the same service or product.
    - Provides an acceptable substitute service or product.

- Provides an incentive/benefit for customers to buy.
- Describe how each of the following five forces creates competition for you.
    - Direct rivals.
    - New companies ready to enter into your business.
    - Substitute products.
    - Customer pressure.
    - Supplier pressure (for example, including labor and subcontractors).

D. Positioning

This describes how customers view your company. They're the experts. You need to talk to customers, and your competitors' customers, to find out. It's not difficult; it just takes some time. The key here is that the customers' perceptions determine this, not you; customers' perceptions about your company create your positioning. So, you need to ask them.

———— Helpful Questions ————

- Describe the results of any customer surveys or queries to determine:
    - Why customers do business with your firm or not.
    - What you do well/poorly.
    - What your competitors do well/poorly.
    - Your image/reputation.
    - How you and your direct rivals are positioned with regard to:
        - Price.
        - Quality.
        - Service.
- Determine if you are positioned as you desire.
    - If so, what might you do to strengthen your position?
    - If no, what might you do to create this desired position?

E. Key customers

Your attention here should be to characterize your customers and determine how to serve them efficiently and effectively. This is important in understanding the influence your customers have, individually and as a group, on your success. You'll be surprised at what you can learn. To paraphrase Yogi Berra: "It's amazing what you see, if you just look."

—————— Helpful Questions ——————

- How many customers do you have?
- What percentage of them comprises 70 to 80 percent of your sales?
- Who are these big customers, and what do they want from you?
- What buying characteristics do these big customers have in common regarding:
  - Price?
  - Quality?
  - Service?
- Are you making money with your smaller customers?
- How can you serve these smaller customers more efficiently?
- Should you "fire" any customers because you can't give them what they want (for example, a too-low price, an employee for them to abuse)?

F. Market opportunities

This describes the possible market opportunities open to the company. These are areas that the company could pursue given its core capabilities, its ability to acquire the required resources, and the availability of willing-to-buy customers.

—————— Helpful questions to help you ——————

- What are the company's specific core competencies?
  - Procedures.
  - Manufacturing/Operations.

- Selling.
- Service.
- Problem-solving.
- In what new work areas could these same skills be used:
  - Right now?
  - With investment in new resources, training, and management?
- Can the company pursue these opportunities without:
  - Diluting its' other efforts?
  - Losing out on better opportunities?
  - Taking on too much risk?

G. Target markets

This describes the opportunities that you're actively going to pursue. It also describes why these make sense (e.g., highest profit, least training required). Take the list of opportunities from before and then carefully consider which of those opportunities you should target for your attention.

——————— Helpful Questions ———————

- Which of the opportunities require minimal:
  - Resources?
  - Training and management attention?
  - Cost increases?
- Which of the opportunities lead to high:
  - Sales?
  - Profits?
- Which of the opportunities are complimentary to current:
  - Operations?
  - Sales and Marketing?
- What will current and future competition be like for each opportunity?
- What are the likely trends for each opportunity?
- Which of the opportunities present the lowest risks?

H. Marketing strategies and goals

This is the key section of the Business Plan. It describes how you'll be successful by describing the specific actions you'll employ to achieve your Vision and Goals. These actions, of course, are influenced by the industry environment, your capabilities, the competitive environment, and the opportunities. So, all the previous analyses will direct you toward your strategies and your ability to set and achieve goals. Use the Spider Diagram from Chapter 2 to help you.

You should first establish the company's strategies in light of all the other information up to this point - what you will do to make the company a success. Then describe the goals, which might include profit and customer-satisfaction measures, to move the company toward your vision. Be crystal clear about all of this and remember that goals have a time or date for completion.

—————————— Helpful Questions ——————————

- Exactly how will you make your sales?
  - Sell old products/services to old customers (least risky).
  - Sell new products/services to old customers.
  - Sell old products/services to new customers.
  - Sell new products/services to new customers (most risky).
- How will you generate your profits?
  - Target sales volume.
  - Target selling price (and rationale).
  - Target decrease in costs (and how achieved).
- What will you do to provide customer satisfaction?
- How will you achieve your desired strategic position?
  - Specific customers.
  - Specific geography.
  - Specific products/services.
  - Specific distribution or marketing channels.
  - Acquisition or merger.
  - Vertical or horizontal integration.

———————————— Helpful Questions ————————————

- What are your target sales?
- What is your profit goal:
    - Overall?
    - By product or service?
- What specific strategic position would you like to achieve?
    - New customers, by name or total number?
    - New territories?
    - New marketing channels and distribution relationships?
- How will you measure customer satisfaction, and what will be your goal here?
- What are your goals for each quarter?
- What are your goals for each year?

I. Resources needed and milestones

This section describes the resources you'll need to accomplish the marketing strategies and attain the goals you established. It includes people and equipment as well as dollars.

———————————— Helpful Questions ————————————

- What tangible assets will you need?
    - Equipment, tools, vehicles.
    - Buildings and land.
- How much working capital will you need?
- What people will you need?
    - Managers.
    - Suppliers.
    - Employees, by type.
- What will each of these items above cost?
- By what date will you need each item?

Hint: It may be helpful to put this information in a table. Make a table for each goal, then list the resources needed, the cost, and the delivery date for each.

J. Sales forecast

This section forecasts sales, often for the next one to three years. It should be realistic and attainable, not just "pie in the sky." These sales figures are also in the financial statements, but many people, especially prospective investors, like to see these in a prominent spot.

—————————— **Helpful Questions** ——————————

- What will total sales be:
  - Each month?
  - Each year?
- What will sales be by any characteristics important to your company such as:
  - Product type?
  - Geography?
  - Major customer or customer group?

K. Customer service

This section describes the methods you'll use to provide good customer service. This is a separate section because in today's marketplace it's very important.

—————————— **Helpful Questions** ——————————

- What corporate commitments will you make regarding customer service?
- How will you measure customer service?
- Do you want your company to be focused on customer service?
  - If so, how will you do that?
  - If not, what will be your commitment level to customer service?

5. Operational plan

A. Operational objectives and actions

This describes the plans of each department, group, or key individual for conducting the business plan successfully. Each of these entities should have their own goals and required actions.

Helpful Questions

- What are the goals of each:
  - Group or department?
  - Key individual?
- How will each goal be met?
  - Specific actions.
  - Deadlines.

B. Management team and organization chart

You should describe, in separate paragraphs, the qualifications of each member of the management team. Also, include an organization chart of the firm.

C. Implementation plans

This section should describe how you intend to make the business plan a success. Is it just a bunch of words, or do you have procedures or policies that ensure your success?

Helpful Questions

- What processes will you implement to reach your goals? For example:
  - A system of managing to attain the goals.
  - Regular meetings with action plans.

- Manager assignments tied to incentives.
  - Accountability and responsibility.
- What incentives will be given for success?
- How will you communicate with everyone?

D. Risks

This describes the things that could go wrong—things that are realistic but possible. For example, sales might be less than you now believe. Describe how this could happen, what the effect would be on the company, and what you'll do if it happens.

——————— Helpful Questions ———————

- What is the likelihood of lower:
  - Sales?
  - Prices?
- What is the likelihood of higher costs?
  - Cost of goods sold?
  - Overhead?
- Why might these events occur?
- What will you do to adjust to these events?
- What external risks might you have and how will you mitigate them?
  - Legal.
  - Regulatory.
  - Financial.
  - Other.

6. Legal and professional issues

Outline the legal issues that are especially important to the business (for example, an environmental clean-up company must adhere to specific health and safety or other regulations). Also outline your team of professional advisors including your banker, attorney, outside accountant, and insurance agent.

─────────────── **Helpful Questions** ───────────────

- What issues are significant to your business? For example:
  - Industry-specific.
  - Regulatory.
  - Health and safety.
  - Standards groups.
  - Technology.
  - Insurance.
- Who are your professional advisors (name, address, phone)?
  - Accountant/financial advisor.
  - Attorney.
  - Banker.
  - Insurance broker.
  - Business coach.

7. Financial plans

This should include your financial performance for the past three years; your projections for the coming year and perhaps the next two years after that, if possible; and your plans to improve your financial performance. Your financial statements should include the balance sheet, the income statement for each year, and a cash flow projection for the coming year. You might also include some financial ratios that are important in your industry or business.

Helpful Questions

- Do you have accurate financial statements?
- If not, what will you do to make them accurate?
- Do you have thoughtful projections?
- Have you determined reasons for your:
  - Financial symptoms?
  - Financial problems?
- Have you determined your needs for funds?
  - Sources of funds?
  - Specific uses for funds?

The interviewing process: one of a manager's most critical activities

Isn't this a job for the HR department?

Virtually all of the firms that we encounter tell us that "our people are our most important resource." It's a wonderful statement, isn't it? If only all these companies acted as if it were true!

Let's focus on the initial step for developing this great resource: interviewing the special people who will become part of your company. What could be more important?

We've found that many companies treat the interview process as if it were a grocery shopping experience. The managers describe the open position in general terms and then leave it up to the HR department to find someone who fits this description. Sometimes these managers have only a single brief discussion with candidates before hiring them. And sometimes the managers never meet the candidates at all before hiring them!

Now let's be clear here. We're not disparaging the HR department in any way. The HR folks have a very key role to play in the interview process, and they can provide tremendous insights and guidance. But the hiring managers are the ones who must take the responsibility for finding the right people who will work for them.

But I'm too busy to do all this

Of course you're too busy. Every manager is too busy. But one of the interesting things we've observed is that managers who cut corners in the interviewing process spend an inordinate amount of time trying to "fix" the folks that they wrongly hired. This leads to either an extended period of remediation or an eventual decision to terminate and start all over again. In either case, managers are diverted from doing what they should be doing: coaching their most talented people to excel.

In fact, many managers spend more time choosing a new restaurant for Saturday night than they do interviewing a new candidate. But a bad meal only gives you indigestion the next day. A bad hire gives you heartburn for weeks or months.

So, what's the answer?

Managers must treat the search for new employees as one of their most important activities. Indeed it is!

Think about the interview process for a minute. If you choose the right people, you have the opportunity to coach them to excellence so they can help you reach your own goals as well as those of the company. If you don't choose the right people, you waste your time and theirs, because you endanger your ability to reach your goals and because you divert the new hires from finding a position in which they could be successful (just may not be in your company).

So, how do I do this?

The hiring manager should work closely with the HR department to identify the skills and natural abilities required by the position and to create a position description, as we described in Chapter 3. Then, the manager must interview candidates with a keen eye to discover those skills and abilities. Talented HR professionals can help identify how to make those discoveries, but the hiring manager should be actively participating in the interview process.

Identifying the natural abilities needed for a particular position (for example, sales manager) is a relatively straightforward activity. Identifying candidates who actually possess those talents, however, is a bit more challenging.

What's different about this approach?

We know that we often can teach a person the knowledge and the skills needed for a particular position. So, if we choose to do so, we can hire a person with the right natural abilities (such as a great sense of responsibility and a love for numbers) and teach that person the skills and knowledge needed (such as how to do accounting in our company).

This is in contrast, of course, with the historical method of choosing folks who seem to have the right experience (such as a good resume) but lack the right attitude or lack some other needed natural ability. With these folks, we bring them on board as a top-quality hire (after all, that resume sure looked good) and then later fire them for incompetence. The truth of the matter, all too frequently, is that we are at fault for putting the person in a role in which they couldn't succeed.

The majority of companies that we've witnessed use a "traditional" approach to interviewing for new employees. They rely very heavily on the candidate's resume to guide their interview and to influence their conclusion regarding the candidate's suitability for the position to be filled.

In fact, we've witnessed too many interviews with candidates that were little more than recitations of the resume. We've even watched professional recruiters operate similarly: go down the resume, line by line, to ask the candidate to say the same thing live and in person.

So, you might ask, what's wrong with that? Don't candidates' past records indicate whether they can do the job? After all, if they've done it before, they can do it again.

First, let's be clear. The resume, if truthful, is a great starting point with regard to the candidate's accomplishments. It's a means of identifying past achievements and a springboard that can lead you to other questions and issues.

But remember that the resume is a marketing document. It is meant to cast the candidate in a very favorable light, and the candidate has had lots of time to revise and tinker with it.

Remember also that you're seeking a truly outstanding individual to take the position that you're seeking to fill. You don't want someone who can "just do the job" because they have, perhaps, done something similar in the past. At least, we hope you don't.

In order for you to find that truly outstanding person, you'll need to look far beyond the resume. We focus on three things that will help you identify a terrific new employee.

First, we use the empowerment model we described in Chapter 3 to guide our process. More specifically, we know that employees can be empowered properly when they:

- Share our principles.
- Are reliable.
- Are competent.

So, we try very hard to construct an interview process that will reveal these three attributes in the candidates we meet. Make no mistake, this is not easy, but the better you can do this, the better your chances of finding that terrific new employee.

Second, we put high emphasis on the natural abilities of the candidate—higher emphasis, many times, than the actual accomplishments as indicated in the resume. We do this because we think that in most cases it's easier to train someone with the right characteristics than it is to attempt to change the natural abilities of someone who has a nice resume.

Candidates with the right natural abilities for their position will make you smile every day. They'll love the job you've assigned them, and they'll require little in the way of management or motivational coaching. Your job is to find those people and be sure they're in the right position, and that requires that you understand their natural abilities.

Third, we develop questions that are specific to the position we are trying to fill—questions that are intended to help identify the natural abilities that we seek for that position. We also create guidance on the answers to those questions, and this may include the way the candidate answers the question as well as the actual content of the answer.

An example

As an illustration, we'll describe how we used the process to assist one of our clients. This example, unlike the general description you just read, is specific to one particular position in one particular company. The questions that you'll develop for a specific position in your company will be different, but we hope that our suggestions here will help you develop those particular questions.

This company was a fast-growing service firm. It had offices around the country, and the entire management team was under pressure to deliver better results each successive quarter.

The company's offices were run by local managers who had total responsibility for sales as well as operations. Unfortunately, only a few of the offices were led by high-performing managers; the majority exhibited mediocre or poor results and high turnover.

The top management of the company was not sure what to do to improve the results at each of the city locations. Some managers were doing great, others were doing poorly, and the management team was stymied in understanding how to get top managers for all the cities.

A 4-step process

We assisted this management team by using the interviewing process described here. Our objective was to identify the natural abilities possessed by the top-performing city managers and then to design a series of questions that would help our client identify those abilities in the candidates they'd interview. This was a four-step process.

Our first step was to talk with the management team about the importance of natural abilities for this key position: city manager. They acknowledged that their "A-Team" city managers (there were six of them out of a total of 17) seemed to have some innate and natural abilities that drove them to success.

The management team acknowledged, however, that they just didn't know how to identify these natural abilities in the candidates that they interviewed for the city manager position. The management team knew that they could teach the day-to-day skills and knowledge that the city managers would need, and they also knew that they couldn't teach the needed natural abilities to those who didn't have them.

Our second step in the process was to interview the six top-performing city managers to determine the natural abilities they possessed. We wanted to know what their secret sauce was—what they naturally brought to the position that enabled them to be so successful.

In preparation for our interview with each of these six city managers, we asked each of them to think hard about two issues. First, what natural abilities did they possess that made them so good in their position? Second, how could we identify those abilities in candidates that crossed our threshold?

Then, several days later, we interviewed them to determine the answers to those two questions. We asked them several questions designed to detect natural abilities ("What activities give you great satisfaction, at work or at home?"). We also had discussions with them to determine how we'd find those natural abilities in others (recognizing that we can't ask candidates if they possess such abilities because they'll simply tell us that they do!).

For step three, we determined the natural abilities that these top-performing city managers had in common. In fact, there were several of them. And in some cases, there was great similarity in the words used by these managers to describe these natural abilities.

The key natural abilities identified by at least three of the six individuals, together with the number of individuals who identified these abilities, were:

(6) **Communicator: love to find things in common, excite customers, read them well, listen to what is important to them.**
(6) **High energy.**
(4) **Goal-oriented.**
(4) **Competitive.**
(3) **Always optimistic or positive.**
(3) **Strong work ethic/sense of responsibility/passion.**

Although not specifically identified by the managers during the interviews, it also became apparent to us that they used humor in their communications. We considered that to be potentially important to the success of these individuals in their role as city managers.

In step four, with great assistance from these city managers, we created some questions and situations that the company then used in its interviews with candidates. We also created annotated answers to these questions, indicating what to look for in the candidates' responses, for each of the natural abilities we identified. In some instances, we could use a simple question, whereas in others we needed to look for a pattern or habit of behavior throughout the interview.

This is, of course, tough stuff. Detecting natural abilities in a candidate is not easy. This approach, however, will greatly increase your chances of identifying the natural abilities that a candidate might possess to excel in the position you are filling.

Please bear in mind that the information here should serve as a starting point for your company. There is no single set of questions that will work for all positions. And there are numerous combinations of natural abilities that could spell success in any given position.

You will, however, be able to refine the process for your company to make it more effective for every position. Remember to start with only your very top performers. The natural abilities that make them successful are very likely different than the natural abilities of the average performers.

Here are the questions we created.

Great Communicator

1. When you go to greet the candidate, indicate that you are finishing up something. Ask him if it's okay that he wait nearby for about 10 to 15 minutes. Leave him in an area where he is proximate to one or two employees who are "clued-in."

Look for: A candidate who readily engages in conversation, and relationship building, with the nearby clued-in employee. He should show a readiness and some real enthusiasm for doing this—it's what we expect him to do when he meets a new customer-prospect.

2. If the candidate was interviewed previously by someone else, ask the candidate to tell you about the person that interviewed her.

Look for: A candidate who can quickly and accurately portray some key characteristics of the company person that previously talked with her. Was she actually listening, and did she really "read" this person, or did she miss the boat?

3. Generally, during the interview:

Look for: A candidate who makes you feel comfortable; a candidate who finds common areas of interest, and who shows an interest in you, the position, or the company.

4. At some point toward the middle or end of your interview session, ask the candidate to describe something that you previously described to him (e.g., the goals expected of them, or the activities they'd conduct).

Look for: A candidate who exhibits strong recall and who obviously has listened carefully to what you've said.

5. Generally, during the interview:

Look for: A candidate to use body language, clarifying questions, and follow-up comments that indicate a natural ability for listening. She shouldn't interrupt repeatedly or try to finish your sentences for you.

<u>High Energy</u>
6. Generally during the interview:

Look for: A candidate who exudes energy. On the phone, you'll notice it (if you listen for it!) in the tone of voice, the enthusiasm, the tone, and the pitch. In person, the candidate may be fidgety, may have a hard time sitting still for long, may use gestures and body language that tell you that he doesn't put his feet on the desk. This is something that is best observed (rather than trying to find questions to ask about it). In the longer run, you'll find some tricks of your own to detect this.

<u>Goal-Oriented</u>
7. Ask the candidate what her goals were last year, whether she met them, and why.

Look for: A candidate who answers quickly (top of mind recall) and specifically about her goals. If she has to think about it, it's probably not a habit, and therefore probably not something she likes to do. Also look for enthusiasm about the <u>process</u> of setting and reaching goals (even if they weren't attained for some good reason!).

8. Ask the candidate how often he sets goals for himself, and to give you examples.

Look for: A candidate who answers quickly (top of mind recall) and specifically about his goal-setting and for a candidate who does this stuff all the time!

<u>Competitive</u>
9. Ask the candidate about her hobbies, interests, and outside activities.

Look for: A candidate who does things that are competitive. The obvious answer is to look for someone who competes in sports, but there are some other very competitive activities such as chess, sailing, theater, and music (e.g., real musicians love to "do it just a little better than the other guy"). Look for these types of activities.

10. Ask the candidate if he's ever won a sales contest, and how he felt about it.

Look for: *A candidate who obviously is excited about winning the contest. You'll hear it in his voice, and if he is sitting nearby you'll see it in his face and his body language. Bear in mind here, you're looking for the <u>way</u> he answers this question more than the answer itself.*

Always Positive

11. Ask the candidate why her last job, and/or the one before that, didn't work out, or why she left.

Look for: *A candidate who doesn't blame others for her failures or life changes. Look for someone who projects a positive light on her past experiences and who assumes responsibility for her choices*

12. Generally, during the interview:

Look for: *A candidate who makes <u>you</u> feel positive: a candidate who smiles, talks in positive terms, and seems optimistic. In some cases, he may even indicate his aversion to negative things (e.g., watching local TV news with its endless litany of negative stories).*

Look for: *A candidate who projected these same qualities when talking with our "waiting room" employees. Is this natural, or is he putting up a front?*

Strong Work Ethic

13. Ask the candidate: "Describe your first work experience."

Look for: *A candidate who had a real job (worked at the grocery store, etc.) at an early age. You might also want to probe the candidate about the benefits that came from this first job to get further hints that this is an ingrained ability.*

<u>Humor</u>

If you think that humor may be a useful natural ability for this position:

14. Ask the candidate when she last used humor with a customer, and to describe the situation.

<u>Look for</u>: *A candidate who replies both quickly and specifically. This is indicative of habitual behavior, and is a clue to her natural abilities. You're trying to determine if she does this as a habit, if it's part of her makeup—a natural ability.*

15. Generally, during the interview:

<u>Look for</u>: *A candidate to use humor with you, or with others during the interview. Is he looking for chances to smile, and to make you smile?*

APPENDIX D

The sales process: An example step

In Chapter 4, we talked about the need to have a sales process. The basic notion is to have a series of steps that best allow you to secure the right customers for your business. These steps should constantly be under development and scrutiny so that you can improve them and so that everyone can borrow the best ideas from each other.

We describe here a fictitious, though plausible, step in a sales process for a company that uses the telephone to make initial contacts with prospective customers. We hope that you'll pay more attention to the spirit and intent of this step than to the actual content. This is because the content will be specific to your organization (you're going to perfect the content for your organization, and we can't do that), whereas the intent is common across similar organizations (those that use the telephone for initial contacts).

We believe that each step of your process should have a clear goal. Then, the process should describe how you'll achieve that goal.

Example Sales Process
First Phone Contact

Goal of this step: to set a face-to-face meeting with potential clients to explain how the benefits of our product will satisfy and even exceed their needs.

- Make a good first impression.
  - Make a list of key points to cover before dialing.

- Smile before you dial. Get yourself in the mood for a positive conversation.
- Use your best introduction. This is something that you should work on continually, to determine what works and what doesn't. ("Hello, Mr. Strauss. This is Jim Little from BBB Computer Services. I was referred to you by Jerry Jellinek, who told me how much he enjoys working with you. [Pause briefly to allow client to respond]. Jerry also said that you may have need of a specialty computer services provider. May I take a few minutes to talk with you?"

- Show interest and excitement.
  - Be interested and upbeat.
  - Use a positive tone of voice.
  - The client can't see your beatific face, only listen to your voice—use it wisely.

- Determine client needs and goals
  - Listen, listen, listen.
    - Use your list of questions and write the client's answers.
    - Use the client's tone and emphasis to explore areas you didn't anticipate.
    - Summarize the client's words to reaffirm that you got the point.
    - Don't sell, don't brag, don't tell the client about you (not yet!).
    - Don't interrupt.
  - Ask leading questions to determine the client's needs and goals.
    - Ask them specifically what their goals are for the project.
    - Ask them specifically what should or shouldn't be done during the project.

- Identify the selection criteria.
  - Ask the client how they will select his provider.
  - Ask enough questions, without interjecting your own opinion, to clarify the emphasis that the client may place on

multiple criteria (for example, the primary consideration is previous experience, the secondary consideration is approach, and price is third).

- Ask for a meeting.
  - Affirm your enthusiasm for the client's project.
  - Indicate that the client's needs are right in line with your skills and experience.
  - Tell the client that you'd like to make a visit in order to demonstrate the benefits you can provide by working on their project.
  - Suggest two dates when you could make the visit and suggest the amount of time you'd like for the visit.
  - Be sure to get the client's permission for your presentation (for example, if you plan to use a projector, be sure that the client has the appropriate room available).
  - Get affirmation of the meeting time, place, and duration before moving to the next step.

- Identify the selection committee (if possible).
  - Ask the client if they will solely decide who will be selected for this project or if other folks will have input on the decision.
    - If the client is the sole decision-maker, indicate that "I know that this decision is an important one, and you have a great deal to consider in your decision. When I visit with you next week, I'll indicate clearly to you how we can meet your goals and needs."
    - If the client is not the sole decision-maker, ask if it is possible that the other decision-makers and/or influencers will be present. Ask the client to give you the names and positions of these folks, and to also explain their relationship to the client.
  - Thank the client for generously taking the time to talk with you. Reaffirm the meeting date and time, and indicate your enthusiasm for meeting with the client.
  - Send any material to the client that you may have promised.

- Keep the list of meeting attendees handy and read it periodically before the meeting. When you go to the meeting, you'll need to know the people and their relationships to each other. (As described in the next step, at the meeting, you should learn their names (match the face to the name) within the first five to 10 minutes so that you can call each person by name. Remember: To most people, no sound is as sweet as their own name).

Improving communications

At least half of all the problems experienced by our clients over the years have been related to "communications." And we have yet to meet a single client that admits to communicating too well!

Everyone knows the Golden Rule: "Do unto others as you would have others do unto you." It's great advice, and many people strive daily to put it into practice. In fact, it's highly intuitive that the effective application of the Golden Rule would improve all of our lives immeasurably.

It's only logical, then, that you should strive to apply this rule to your communications with others. After all, if you "communicate with others as you would have others communicate with you," things should go fine, right?

Well, unfortunately, no—it's not right. And that's because no one is like you. Quite simply, other people hear, process, and respond to information in ways that are different from the way that you do.

The jury paradox

If you've ever served on a jury, you've seen this firsthand. Twelve individuals all hear, see, and otherwise experience the same information at the same time from the same vantage point. Yet the ensuing deliberations would lead an objective outsider to conclude that some of the jury members must have experienced something significantly different than the other members.

These differences sometimes prompt us to conclude that others aren't listening to us, or that they simply are wrong in their analysis and conclusions. After all, when we gathered the information, we came to our own correct conclusion, so why didn't the others do so as well?

Humans are like radios

To gain some insight into this dilemma, imagine that you operate a radio station and that you send your signal out at 97.5. If one of your potential listeners has a radio tuned to 103.5, she won't receive your signal. It won't matter how loud you broadcast or how fast you talk; she simply won't hear you.

Now imagine that the person with whom you're communicating, in a face-to-face discussion, is also a radio. His brain is the biological equivalent of the radio tuning knob! You're job, then, is to figure out what "frequency" he uses to receive messages so that you can broadcast effectively.

So how do you do this? First, throw out the Golden Rule!

Instead, "Communicate with others as they wish to have you communicate with them." In other words, find their frequency: Determine how they receive and process information and tailor your approach, style, and content to fit their needs.

How difficult is this? Actually, it's very easy in concept but very difficult in practice—something that we consider to be a high-level skill.

Nevertheless, as soon as you view others as unique receivers, you'll already have improved your ability to communicate. You can even make it a game or a challenge: How quickly can I find their frequency? Should I speak slowly or fast, be calm or animated, listen first or dive in…?

In their own way, through words, body language, tone of voice, and other means, the other person will let you know if you're on the right frequency. Your job is to read the signals.

Why is this so difficult just because I've added a few folks?

Let's look first at why it's so difficult to communicate well, even if you want to do so and even if you've solved the "frequency riddle." Imagine that you and I are the only ones in your company. There is a single line of communication between us; after all, no one else is around.

Now let's assume that another person, Ken, joins your firm. Now there are four lines of communication, or "chat groups": you to me, you to Ken, Ken to me, and all three of us in one chat group. It's already become disproportionately difficult to keep everyone well informed. It certainly was easier when there were only two of us.

Now imagine that there are 20 of us in the firm. There are now approximately one million lines of communication! If we add a single additional employee, to reach 21, that jumps to approximately two million lines of communication. In effect, the addition of each employee doubles the number of lines of communication. By the time you reach 30 employees, you'll have hit one billion.

You can see that having just 20 employees presents you with an impossible challenge. It's just not feasible to try to keep everyone informed about all the issues of your organization of 20 people. Imagine the difficulties in an organization of 300, or 3,000, or 30,000, or more.

Sure, you knew that communicating well with everyone wasn't easy, but the numbers here illustrate this isn't something that will be cured with more meetings. It's just flat-out impossible to do it!

So, how do we fix it?

We don't! Faced with the reality of this math, we know that we can't fix this problem; we can't keep everyone informed on all the issues. Instead, our intent should be to communicate to each employee the information he needs to achieve his goals. The extraneous stuff is the fluff that bogs employees down.

The way to communicate this goal-focused information, of course, is to follow a management system like the one we described in Chapter 6. At a minimum, you should conduct a regular (monthly at least) GMT meeting that focuses on plan-versus-actual for the company, conduct weekly one-on-one meetings that focus on individual goals, and instill a culture that values goal attainment and accountability.

Quite simply, you and your staff must learn to live with imperfect communication. Make it clear to everyone that it's impossible for them to know about everything that's happening (even though some of them really want to know this!).

But make it just as clear that you have a system in place that will provide them with the information they need to achieve their goals. They'll love that part.

Recommended Reading

We recommend the following books to you. Some of them provide in-depth background information on key topics discussed here, and others are simply valuable resources for managers.

Built to Last, by James Collins and Jerry Porras, HarperBusiness, 1994. This book describes what makes truly exceptional companies different from other companies.

The Checklist Manifesto, by Atul Gawande, Metropolitan Books, 2009. Atul Gawande makes a compelling case for instituting simple checklists when repetitive activities are complex. He illustrates the success of this approach by looking at the airline industry and the healthcare environment.

Competitive Strategy, by Michael Porter, The Free Press, 1980. This now-classic text by a Harvard professor is a guidebook on understanding markets and creating effective strategies for any company. It is the basis of the five-forces model for the competitive environment described here.

Crucial Conversations—Tools for Talking When Stakes are High, by Kerry Patterson, Joseph Grenny, Ron McMillan, and Al Switzler, McGraw Hill, 2002. This book provides tools to increase the quality of dialogues and to avoid "the void created by the failure to communicate [which] is soon filled with poison, drivel, and miscommunication."

The Customer Driven Company, by Richard Whiteley, Addison-Wesley Publishing Company, 1991. This classic on customer service contains numerous examples, cases, and tools for use by any company. It's filled with great ideas.

Customers for Life, by Carl Sewell and Paul Brown, Pocket Books, 1998. Starting with his Ten Commandments of Customer Service, the authors provide guidance on creating outstanding customer service and long-time loyal customers.

Developing the Leader Within You, by John C. Maxwell, Injoy, Inc., 1993.
This book describes five levels of leadership, with tips and guidance on how to progress to the highest level.

The Discipline of Market Leaders, by Michael Treacy and Fred Wiersema, Perseus Books, 1997.
This book provides detailed guidance on how a company can "choose your customers, narrow your focus, and dominate your market." A key theme here is the choice of a generic strategy, and this book was an important resource for our discussion in Chapter 2.

Endurance: Shackelton's Incredible Voyage, by Alfred Lansing, Carroll & Graf Publishers, Inc., 1959.
This is one of the most astonishing survival stories of all time, and an outstanding example of great leadership, picking the right people, and creating new plans to suit changing conditions.

Execution, by Larry Bossidy and Ram Charan, Crown Business, 2002. These authors describe how to build an effective operating process in a company. This ensures that specific actions will be taken, with assigned accountability, to achieve the company's strategies.

First, Break All the Rules, by Marcus Buckingham and Curt Coffman, Simon & Schuster, 1999.
This book emphasizes the important role of the manager as a coach, and it stresses the critical nature of talent and putting people with the right talent in the appropriate roles.

Flight of the Buffalo, by James Belasco and Ralph Stayer, Warner Books, 1993.
These authors advise us on how to create a focused and flexible company with increased productivity, in part by empowering employees to assume increased responsibility. This book was a source for the one-on-one discussions described in Chapter 6.

Focus—The Future of Your Company Depends Upon It, by Al Reis, HarperBusiness, 1996.
The author advises that companies focus on core products, and discard extraneous ones, in order to evolve and increase market share.

The Goal, by Eliyahu M. Goldratt and Jeff Cox, The North River Press, 1992.
This book focuses on overcoming the bottlenecks that inevitably occur in manufacturing processes. The overriding theme, the need to define the right goals for a company—is applicable to any business.

Good to Great, by James Collins, HarperBusiness, 2001.
This research-driven book describes the reasons that cause a company to move from good to great. It focuses on large public companies.

The Great Game of Business, by Jack Stack, Doubleday, 1992.
This book is an entertaining story of how to run your business by keeping financial score, rewarding the team for reaching its goals, and having fun. It is a key source for the reward program described in Chapter 6.

The Illustrated Longitude, by Dava Sobel and William J.H. Andrewes, Walker and Company, 1998.
This interesting book describes the long and arduous challenge faced by seafarers for determining their position on the globe. It is the source for the account of the Scilly Isles tragedy described in Chapter 6.

The Leader in You, by Dale Carnegie & Associates, Inc., Pocket Books, 1993
This book is an easy-to-read account of the time-tested principles of human relations. It can be used by any manager to harness creativity and enthusiasm and create a more productive workplace.

Now, Discover Your Strengths, by Marcus Buckingham and Donald Clifton, The Free Press, 2001.
This book demonstrates how to develop your unique talents and strengths, and those of the people you manage. It stresses the importance of talent in achieving excellence.

Nuts! Southwest Airlines' Crazy Recipe for Business and Personal Success, by Kevin Freiberg and Jackie Freiburg, Broadway Books, 1996.
This book demonstrates how a company practicing principle-centered leadership principles can create a wildly successful company with loyal employees and customers. It also provides insight on how Southwest relentlessly created a low-cost structure.

The One Minute Manager, by Kenneth Blanchard and Spencer Johnson, William Morrow and Company, 1982.
This book outlines a quick and effective program for setting and managing the achievement of goals.

Positioning: The Battle for Your Mind, by Al Reis and Jack Trout, Warner Books, 1986
This is a very easy-to-understand book that clearly illustrates the importance of positioning. Although some of the examples in this book are sometimes dated, the principles of positioning are solidly anchored.

The 7 Habits of Highly Effective People, by Stephen Covey, A Fireside Book, 1989.
This landmark book still provides exceptionally relevant guidance to anyone seeking to increase their effectiveness. For company owners and managers, Covey's principle-centered approach provides real tools for coping with challenging issues and an ever-changing environment.

Soar with Your Strengths, by Donald Clifton and Paula Nelson, Dell Publishing, 1992.
This book advises us to focus on strengths (including natural abilities) and manage weaknesses, and thus increase productivity and performance.

The 21 Indispensable Qualities of a Leader, by John C. Maxwell, Nelson Business, 1999.
John Maxwell advocates that leaders must develop character qualities from the inside out. He presents 21 qualities that he believes all great leaders share.

The 22 Immutable Laws of Marketing, by Al Ries and Jack Trout, HarperBusiness, 1994.
This book contains numerous examples, some a bit dated, that illustrate the author's 22 laws in easy-to-read and clear prose. We've always liked this book.

The Ultimate Question—Driving Good Profits and True Growth, by Fred Reichheld
This book is centered on a single question used to measure the state of customer satisfaction and proactively fixing problems: "Would you recommend us to a friend?"

Zapp! The Lightning of Empowerment, by William C. Byham and Jeff Cox, Fawcett Columbine, 1998.
Zapp! demonstrates how to empower and energize employees, who then will drive the business to higher success and performance.

Index

A

Abilities, natural, 77-78, 89, 91-92

Accountability, 174

Accounts receivable, 204-205

Action steps, 181-186, 190

Apple, 119-120

Audi, 21-22

B

BMW, 119-120

Boundaries, 148-156

Business plan outline, 53-54, 208-209

Business plan, 43-72, 207-223

Business Planning Map, 65-66, 209

Buy-in, 174

C

Calvin Klein, 119-120

Changes, 32-33

Cioffi, Andrew, 96-97

Clarity, 174

Coaching, 96-102

Commitment, 174

Communication, 174, 239-241

Company culture, 140-41

Company deficiencies, 55, 59-60

Company strengths, 55, 59-60

Company-wide reward program, 191-195

Competency, 158, 165-168

Competition, 55, 59-60

Conditions for empowerment, 156-168

Cool Hand Luke, 190

Customer Driven Company, The, 17

Customer-related goals, 31-32

Customers, 109-141

Customers, potential, 131-132

D

Daily huddle, 189-191

Darwin, 69

Declaration of Independence, 19

Defining the position, 81-89

Direction, 171

Discipline, 69

Discounts, 198-200

E

80/20 Rule, 113

Eisenhower, Dwight, 46-47

Employee focus, 94-95, 97

Empowerment, 143-170

F

Financial health goals, 29-31

Financial statements, 197-205

Focus, 94-95, 97

G

GE, 96

GMT meetings, 180-186

Goal management team (GMT), 177-195

Goals, 15-42, 81-83, 99, 148-156, 172, 180, 192

Goals, meetings and, 176-177

Goals, strategies and, 60-64

Golden Goose, the, 29, 31

Golden Rule, the, 239, 240

H

Hamster wheel, 40-41

Honda, 120-121

HR department, 225

Huddle, daily, 189-191

I

Ideas, survival of the fittest, 69-71

Individual goals, 33-41

Industry forces, 55, 59-60

Information, identifying, 52-57

Interviewing process, 225-234

Inventory Days, 203

Inventory, 201-204

J

Johnson and Johnson, 21-22

Jordan, Michael, 80

K

Kelleher, Herb, 88

Kennedy, John F., 62, 63

Kodak, 56, 82

L

Leads, 131-135

Life cycle of a manager,
145-146, 149

Loans, 200

Lombardi, Vince, 96

Low-cost providers, 115-119

M

Management styles, 97-99

Management system, 172-195

Manager focus, 94-95, 97

Manager, life cycle of a,
145-146, 149

Meetings, goals and, 176-177

Miracle, 101

N

Natural abilities, 77-78, 89, 91-92

Near-term goals, 24-29

O

One-on-ones, 188-189

Operations processes, 135-140

Optimism, 77-78

P

People management, 146-147

People, the right, 75-81, 89-96

Pike Place Market, 110-111, 136

Planning process, 49-69

Planning, 43-72

Position description, 83-88, 188, 226

Position, defining the, 81-89

Potential customers, 131-132

Principles, shared, 158-162

Process, the sales, 133-135

Processes, operations, 135-140

Profit, 197-205

Progress, 41

R

Reliability, 158 162-165

Responsibility, 174

Resumes, 103-107, 227

Rewards, 191-195

Robbins, Liz, 194

Robbins, Royal, 15-16, 24, 194

S

Sales Funnel, 129-132

Sales process, the, 133-135

Shared principles, 158-162

Showvell, Sir Clowdisley, 178

Sole proprietorship, 111

Southwest Airlines, 88

Spider Diagram, 59-63, 66, 68, 129

Strategic goals, 32-33

Strategies, customers and, 115-129

Strategies, goals and, 60-64

Strategies, modifying, 64-66

Styles, management, 97-99

Survival of the fittest ideas, 69-71

SWOT analysis, 55-56

T

Team resourcing, 186

Time, 171

Truthfulness, 106

Tylenol, 21-22

V

Vision, 17-24, 34-38, 81-83

W

Welch, Jack, 96

Whiteley, Richard, 17

Z

Xerox, 82-83

About the Authors

John Cioffi is a partner in GoalMakers Management Consultants, a firm that coaches its corporate clients to define and accomplish their goals. John received his first business education growing up in his family's restaurant and lodging business, where he learned customer relations and management at an early age. He then held management positions in firms whose work included toxicological evaluations, economic cost-benefit analysis, industrial hygiene, laboratory analysis, and environmental cleanup, and he went on to run a subsidiary of a Fortune 100 company. He has been an executive business coach and a mergers and acquisitions intermediary for 15 years, assisting business owners across the country in creating, and in some cases selling, their successful businesses.

John has written business articles for numerous publications, and given seminars and speeches around the country on business planning, mergers and acquisitions, and financial management. He received his undergraduate degree from Colby College, a master's degree from Dartmouth, and an MBA from the Wharton School. He lives in the rural environs of Seattle with his wife, Amy, and their two llamas, two goats, and two dogs. He enjoys playing soccer and tennis, hiking, and photography.

Ken Willig, who is a high-energy businessman, entrepreneur, author, management consultant, and coach of America's CEOs, was the founding partner of GoalMakers Management Consultants. He has founded, directed, developed, and sold numerous successful businesses. He has been a successful entrepreneur throughout his career, starting with the founding of a heavy construction equipment company at age 28 in Los Angeles, and its subsequent sale to Clark Equipment. Ken founded two banks in Southern California. He and the famous actor John Wayne founded the John Wayne Tennis Club in Newport Beach. Ken is the only person that Wayne ever allowed to use his name on a commercial venture. Ken has also been president and headmaster of a K through 12 Christian school. He was on the ground floor of the cellular phone business and in 1987 won national recognition as the Entrepreneur of the Year for his achievements in founding, developing, and growing a national chain of cellular telecommunication retail centers. Subsequently, he developed and directed the MBA Entrepreneurship program at City University in Seattle. Ken attended Purdue University where he earned a BS in mechanical engineering. He lives in Scottsdale with his wife, Noreen. They have six children and 13 grandchildren.

Your Comments

We would love to hear your comments on *6 Habits of Highly Successful Managers*. We wrote this book hoping that it would provide you with:

- Reliable information.
- Useful and illustrative anecdotes.
- Ideas that you can apply right away.
- Clear and unambiguous explanations.
- A tone that is neither too academic nor too casual.

You can contact us with your comments at
johnc@goalmakers.com
kenw@goalmakers.com

Please also visit us at
www.goalmakers.com